TOBACCO TINS
TINS *and Their Prices*

LATEST PRICES

AL BERGEVIN

Cover Design: Ann Eastburn
Interior Layout: Anthony Jacobson
Photographs: A. J. Bergevin

Library of Congress Catalog
Card Number 86-050132

ISBN 0-87069-464-2

Copyright © 1986
Wallace-Homestead Book Company

10 9 8 7 6 5 4 3

Published by

Wallace-Homestead Book Company
201 King of Prussia Road
Radnor, Pennsylvania 19089

Wallace-Homestead Book Company is part of
ABC Consumer Magazines, Inc.,
One of the ABC Publishing Companies.

Contents

Acknowledgments

I would like to thank the following people for their help in putting this book together. Without them this book could not have been done. And a very special thanks to those who wished to remain unnamed.

Millie Vacarella
St. Paul, Minnesota

Eric Vacarella
St. Paul, Minnesota

A. J. Bergevin
Mesa, Arizona

Ray Rosenberger
Lakeland, Minnesota

Steve Stumpf
Lakeland, Minnesota

Introduction

The popularity of collecting tin containers has grown dramatically in the past five years. Antiques dealers all agree that collectors, decorators, and designers have created a great demand for these interesting and colorful "artifacts."

Because of the enormous variety of tin containers, this book covers only cigar, cigarette, and pipe tobacco containers. But it contains approximately one-half of the tobacco tins known to be in existence.

The most important factor to consider when purchasing a tin is its condition. (See the "Guide to Grading.") Condition is followed in importance by rarity and age. The collector buying the item should see the actual condition before he or she purchases it.

There are pros and cons on whether or not to restore or touch up a tin container. From the standpoint of an antiques dealer, tins should be cleaned but not touched up before they are sold. A collector may wish to have a tin restored for his or her own collection. But, unless you are an expert at restoration, do not attempt to touch up a tin yourself. I would never attempt it. Leave it to the experts. Never use lacquer on a tin, because it will discolor the tin and will eventually crack. When cleaning a tin do not use hot or even warm water, because this will probably destroy the color. I have achieved the best and safest results with cool water, a soft rag, and a mild bar soap such as Ivory.

The prices shown in this book are based on the current asking prices for tins that are in excellent condition. Prices may vary from dealer to dealer. It is important to remember that this is a price *guide* not a price list.

The serious collector would be wise to join the TCCA (Tin Container Collectors Association), 11650 Riverside Drive, North Hollywood, CA 91602. Also, a book by David Griffith, *Decorative Printed Tins,* has an excellent history of tin lithography that can supply answers to questions the technically-minded collector may have.

I hope this book helps you in your continuing search for one of America's most beautiful art forms—tin containers.

Guide to Grading

Scale of 5 to 1

5   **Mint:** Brand-new condition.
4   **Near-Mint:** Only slight signs of use.
3   **Excellent:** Minor blemish, no rust.
2   **Good:** Minor scratching and fading, minor stains.
1   **Fair:** Scratches, some fading, some rust spots, minor dents.

All prices in this book are for items in Near-Mint condition, regardless of the condition of example pictured.

Cigar Containers

Unless otherwise noted, the cigar containers pictured in this section all feature lithographed tin labels. For easy reference, all of the tins in this book appear in alphabetical order within their category.

Advance Agent, round, 6 × 4½ inches, **$40.**

Advance Agent, horizontal box, 8 × 6 × 4 inches, **$100.**

Aire Dale, round, paper label, 6 × 5 inches, **$45.**

All American, round, 6 × 4 inches, **$75.**

7

Alone, vertical box, 6×5×4 inches, **$20.**

Alone, horizontal box, 4×3×1 inches, **$10.**

American Sweets, vertical box, 6×3×3 inches, **$35.**

Bank Note, vertical box, 6×3×3 inches, **$22.**

Banquet Hall, square flat, 3×3×¼ inches, **$25.**

Bengal, square flat, $2\frac{1}{2} \times 2\frac{1}{2} \times \frac{1}{4}$ inches, **$18.**

Ben Franklin, vertical box, $6 \times 3 \times 3$ inches, **$35.**

Between the Acts, horizontal box, $5 \times 2 \times 1$ inches, **$10.**

Between the Acts, horizontal box, $5 \times 2 \times 1$ inches, **$12.**

Bill William, horizontal box, $5 \times 4 \times 1$ inches, **$20.**

Big Value, vertical box, $6 \times 3 \times 3$ inches, **$20.**

Big Wolf, vertical box, $6 \times 2 \times 2$ inches, paper label, **$25.**

Big Wolf, vertical box, paper label, $4 \times 4 \times 6$ inches, **$35.**

Bison, vertical box, $6 \times 6 \times 3$ inches, **$225.**

Black Fox, round, 6×4 inches, **$325.**

Black Sheep, wallet, $6 \times 2 \times \frac{1}{2}$ inches, **$75.**

Blue Jay, oval, paper label, $6 \times 6 \times 4$ inches, **$65.**

Blue Jay, vertical box, 5½ × 3 × 3, **$100**.

Boldt's Specials, wallet, 6 × 2½ × ½ inches, **$25**.

Bougher's, round, 5 × 3 inches, **$20**.

Brown Beauties, vertical box, 6 × 3 × 3 inches, **$400**.

Bull Durham, vertical box, paper label, 5 × 3 × 3 inches, **$200**.

Buster Brown, round, 6×4½ inches, **$700.**

Cadet, round, 6×4½ inches, **$45.**

Camel, vertical box, 5×4×2 inches, **$25.**

Cadet, round, 6×3 inches, **$45.**

Camerettes, horizontal box, 2½×1×½ inches, **$20.**

Canadian Club, horizontal box, $4 \times 3 \times 1$ inches, **$15.**

Chance, round, 6×3 inches, **$30.**

Chamber Commerce, horizontal box, $4 \times 2 \times 1$ inches, **$18.**

Chancellor, horizontal box, $3 \times 2 \times 1$ inches, **$10.**

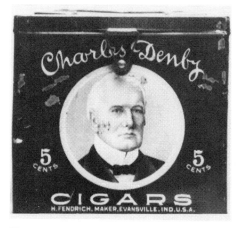

Charles Denby, lunch box, $8 \times 6 \times 6$ inches, **$75.**

Charles Thomson, vertical box, 6×4×4 inches, **$50.**

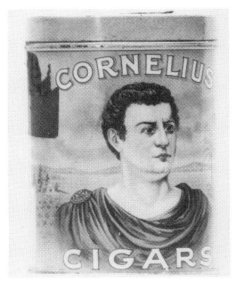

Cornelius, round, 6×3 inches, **$35.**

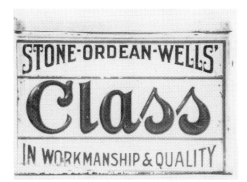

Class, horizontal box, 6×5×3 inches, **$25.**

Counsellor, vertical box, 6×2×2 inches, **$50.**

Club House, horizontal box, 4×3×1 inches, **$12.**

Court Royal, vertical box, $6 \times 2 \times 2$ inches, **$25.**

Cremo, horizontal box, $6 \times 5 \times 2$ inches, **$25.**

Crow-Mo Smokers, lunch box, $7 \times 5 \times 4$ inches, **$100.**

Cuban Seal, horizontal box, $4 \times 3 \times 1$ inches, **$10.**

Cupid Bouquet, square flat, $3 \times 3 \times \frac{1}{4}$ inches, **$45.**

Custom House, round, paper and lithographed label, 6×5 inches, **$45.**

Cute, square flat, 3×3×¼ inches, **$15.**

Dianora, horizontal box, 4½×3×1 inches, **$15.**

Cyana, horizontal box, 4×3×1 inches, **$25.**

Do-U-No, oval, cardboard, 5×4 inches, **$70.**

Daily Double, round, 6×3 inches, **$35.**

Drummond, square flat, 3×3×¼ inches, **$12.**

Dubonnet, horizontal box, $4 \times 3 \times 1\frac{1}{2}$ inches, **$20.**

Dutch Masters, horizontal box, $4 \times 3 \times 1$ inches, **$10.**

Elektra, horizontal box, $4 \times 3 \times 1$ inches, **$20.**

El Rio Rey, round, 5×3 inches, **$35.**

El Roi-Tan, horizontal box, $4 \times 3 \times 1$ inches, **$12.**

El Teano, horizontal box, $4 \times 3 \times 1$ inches, **$18.**

El Verso, horizontal box, $4 \times 2 \times 1$ inches, **$18.**

Emerson, horizontal box, $4\frac{1}{2} \times 2\frac{1}{2} \times 1\frac{1}{2}$ inches, **$14.**

Emilia Garcia, round, 6×4 inches, **$30.**

Emilia Garcia, round, $6 \times 4\frac{1}{2}$ inches, **$15.**

Federal Judge, vertical box, $6 \times 2 \times 2$ inches, **$45.**

Flick & Flock, vertical box, 6×6×4 inches, **$200.**

Flor de Franklin, vertical box, 6×2×2 inches, **$75.**

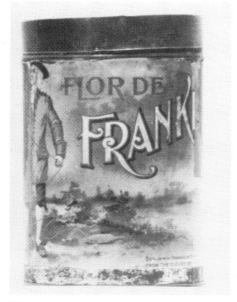

Flor de Franklin, round, paper label, 5×3 inches, **$40.**

Floral Gem, square flat, 3×3×¼ inches, **$30.**

Flor de Leon, round, 6 × 5 inches, **$25.**

Frat, square flat, 3 × 3 × ¼ inches, **$15.**

Fox Trot, round, 7 × 4 inches, **$100.**

Ginks, vertical box, 6 × 2 × 2 inches, **$25.**

Good Cheer, mug, 3×3 inches, **$60.**

Golden Rod, square flat, 2½ × 2½ × ¼ inches, **$15.**

Gobblers, round, 6×4½ inches, **$100.**

Green Turtle, lunch box, 6×5×4 inches, **$100.**

Golden Eagle, square flat, 3×3×¼ inches, **$15.**

Green Turtle, horizontal box, 6×4×3 inches, **$100.**

Half Spanish, round, 6×3 inches, **$45.**   Happy, round, 5×5 inches, **$90.**

Hand Made, round, 8×6 inches, **$12.**   Harvester Kiddies, oval, 5×6½×2½ inches, **$90.**

Harvard Twist, horizontal box, 18×6×1 inches, **$80.**

Hauptmann's Panetela, horizontal box, 5×5×½ inches, **$25.**

S.O.S., round, 6×5 inches, **$25.**

Honest Leaf, round, 6×5 inches, **$80.**

Henry George, vertical box, paper label, 6×3×3 inches, **$20.**

Henry James, vertical box, 6×3×3 inches, **$20.**

His Master's Choice, vertical box, paper label, 6×5×4 inches, **$60.**

Home Run Stogie, round, 6×3 inches, **$375.**

Home Run, round, 6×3 inches, **$1,000 +.**

Hudson, horizontal box, 4×2×1 inches, **$10.**

Izaak Walton, round, 6×5 inches, **$35.**

Hunter, vertical box, paper label, 5½×3×1 inches, **$22.**

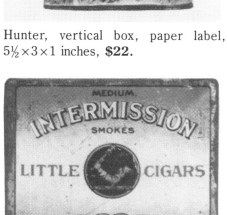

Intermission, square flat, 2½×2½×¼ inches, **$10.**

Izaak Walton, horizontal box, 4×3×1 inches, **$20.**

John Hornick, vertical box, paper label, 6×2×2 inches, **$12.**

John Ruskin, vertical box, $6 \times 2 \times 2$ inches, **$25.**

King Bee, round, 6×3 inches, **$22.**

John Storm, vertical box, $6 \times 4 \times 4$ inches, **$50.**

King Dutch, vertical box, $6 \times 4 \times 4$ inches, **$50.**

Justrite, horizontal box, $5 \times 3 \times 1$ inches, **$15.**

King Midas, vertical box, 5×6×4 inches, **$75.**

La Fendrich, horizontal box, 4×3×1 inches, **$16.**

La Costa, horizontal box, paper label, 4×3×1 inches, **$10.**

La Mavita, vertical box, 6×5×5 inches, **$25.**

Lady Churchill, horizontal box, 5×3×1 inches, **$10.**

La Muna, horizontal box, $6 \times 3 \times 1$ inches, **$25.**

Lipschutz 44, vertical box, $6 \times 2 \times 2$ inches, **$20.**

Le Roy, vertical pocket, $4 \times 2 \times \frac{1}{2}$ inches, **$75.**

Little Barrett, vertical box, 4×2×2 inches, **$45.**

Little Bobbie, horizontal box, 4×3×1 inches, **$20.**

Little Mozart, horizontal box, 7×4×2 inches, **$50.**

Little Story, horizontal box, paper label, 4×3×1 inches, **$20.**

Little Tom, horizontal box, 3×2×1 inches, **$12.**

Louisville Perfectos, vertical box, 6×2×2 inches, **$25.**

Lyceum, square flat, 2½ × 2½ × ¼ inches, **$25.**

Marshall Field, horizontal box, 4 × 3 × 1 inches, **$25.**

Lyceum, horizontal box, 2½ × 1 × ¾ inches, **$10.**

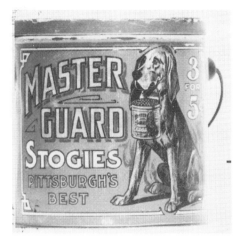

Master Guard, pail, 6 × 5 inches, **$375.**

Mapacuba, vertical box, 4 × 4 × 5 inches, **$35.**

Masterpiece, square flat, 3 × 3 × ¼ inches, **$15.**

Mercantile, horizontal box, $4 \times 3 \times 1$ inches, **$10.**

Maude Hale, vertical box, paper label, $6 \times 2 \times 2$ inches, **$25.**

Merry & Happy, horizontal box, $5 \times 5 \times 1$ inches, **$25.**

Mi-Dia, horizontal box, paper label, $4 \times 3 \times 1$ inches, **$10.**

Melrose, vertical box, $5 \times 3 \times 3$ inches, **$40.**

Tiger cylindrical container, 14 × 8 inches, **$75.**

Ojibwa tobacco, 7×5 inches, **$225.**

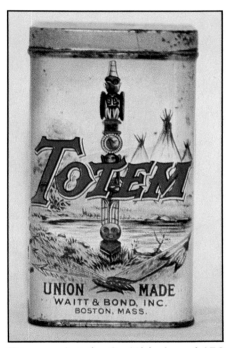

Totem pocket tin, 3×1½ inches, **$450.**　Orcico cigar tin, 6×6×4 inches, **$140.**

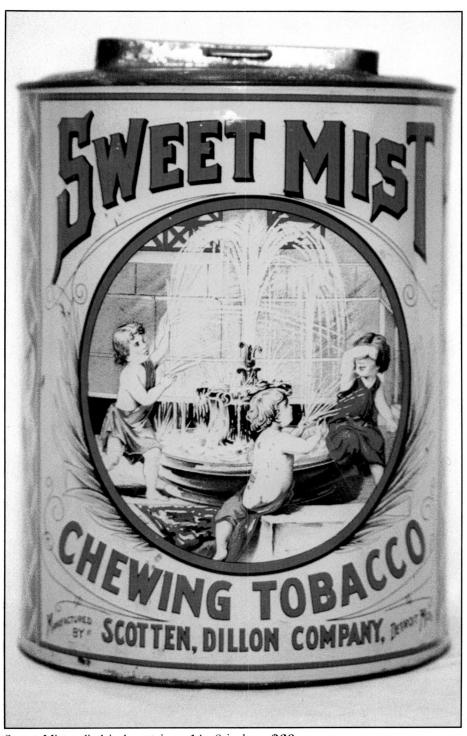

Sweet Mist cylindrical container, 14 × 8 inches, **$60.**

Dixie Queen cylindrical container, 6×3 inches, **$140.**

Game store tin, 24×10×12 inches, **$450.**

Brother Jonathan cylindrical container, 18×12 inches, **$1,500.**

Sure Shot store tin, 20×8×6 inches, **$250.**

Rock Castle pocket tin, 3½ × 2½ inches, **$450.**

Union Leader pocket tin, 4 × 2 inches, **$30.**

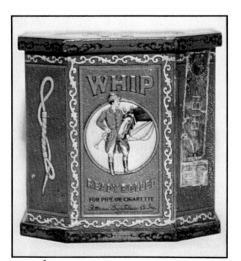

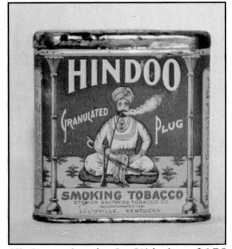

Whip octagonal shape, 6 × 4 inches, **$200.**

Hindoo pocket tin, 3 × 2½ inches, **$150.**

Stag horizontal box, 5×5×5 inches, **$50.**

Cardinal pocket tin, 4×2 inches, **$550.**

Sunset Trail cigar container, 6×6×4 inches, **$195.**

Possum cylindrical container, 6×4½ inches, **$50.**

Sterling cylindrical container, 14×8 inches, **$40.**

Milltown, horizontal box, 6 × 6 × 4 inches, **$100.**

National, vertical box, 6 × 6 × 4 inches, **$25.**

Mozart Habana, horizontal box, 4 × 2½ × 1 inches, **$10.**

New Bachelor, vertical box, 5 × 4 × 2 inches, **$50.**

Muriel, round, 6 × 5 inches, **$20.**

New Bachelor, round, 6 × 3 inches, **$100.**

41

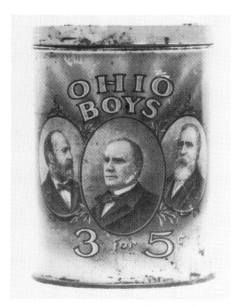

Ohio Boys, round, 6×3 inches, **$300.**

Old King Cole, round, paper label, 5×4 inches, **$800.**

Old Glory, round, 5×5 inches, **$35.**

Old Man's Choice, round, paper label, 6×3 inches, **$25.**

Old Seneca, round, 6×3 inches, **$100.**

Our Monogram, round, 6×3 inches, **$25.**

Opinion, vertical box, 8×4×4 inches, **$25.**

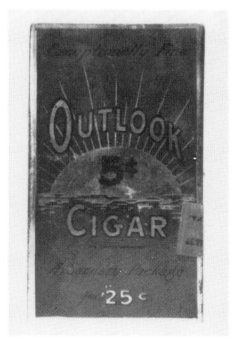

Outlook, wallet, 5×2×½ inches, **$35.**

Pets, square flat, $3 \times 3 \times \frac{1}{4}$ inches, **$8.**

Owl Brand, vertical box, $6 \times 2 \times 2$ inches, **$25.**

Oxford Gems, horizontal box, $6 \times 5 \times 4$ inches, **$45.**

Pippins, vertical box, $5 \times 2 \times 2$ inches, **$40.**

Parisiana, horizontal box, $6 \times 4 \times 1\frac{1}{2}$ inches, **$25.**

Pom Pom, horizontal box, $8 \times 5 \times 2$ inches, **$10.**

Popper's Ace, vertical box, $7 \times 5 \times 5$ inches, **$85.**

Popper's Ace, oval, 5×3 inches, **$250.**

Portina, square flat, $2\frac{1}{2} \times 2\frac{1}{2} \times \frac{1}{4}$ inches, **$10.**

Popper's Ace, vertical box, $6 \times 3 \times 3$ inches, **$150.**

Possum, round, 6×4½ inches, **$50.**

Press Club, horizontal box, 4×3×1 inches, **$25.**

Provana, vertical box, 6×2×2 inches, **$22.**

Que Placer, horizontal box, 4×3×1 inches, **$12.**

Recollection, horizontal box, 4×2×1 inches, **$15.**

Red Feather, round, 6×4 inches, **$30.**

Red Dot, horizontal box, $4 \times 2 \times 1$ inches, **$12**.

Richman's, vertical box, $4 \times 4 \times 4$ inches, **$25**.

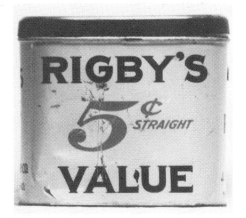

Rigby's, vertical box, $6 \times 5 \times 4$ inches, **$25**.

Robert Burns, horizontal box, $4 \times 3\frac{1}{2} \times 1$ inches, **$25**.

Robert Emmes, trunk, paper label, $6 \times 4 \times 2$ inches, **$22**.

Roosevelt, horizontal box, $4 \times 3 \times 1$ inches, **$30**.

Roxy King, vertical box, 6 × 2 × 2 inches, **$35.**

Royal Gold, vertical box, paper label, 6 × 3 × 1 inches, **$20.**

Scottie, vertical box, 5 × 4 × 4 inches, **$100.**

Scotty, square flat, 3 × 3 × ¼ inches, **$20.**

Seal of Minneapolis, horizontal box, paper label, 4 × 3 × 1 inches, **$15.**

Shamrock, horizontal box, paper label, 4 × 3 × 1 inches, **$20.**

Spanish Lassie, vertical pocket, 4 × 2½ inches, **$45.**

Sight Draft, wallet, 3 × 6 × ½ inches, **$35.**

St. Leger, square flat, 3 × 3 × ¼ inches, **$15.**

St. Leger, square flat, 3 × 3 × ¼ inches, **$12.**

49

Stogie Panetelas, vertical box, 7×4×4 inches, **$20.**

Sunstar, vertical box, paper label, 6×3×3 inches, **$20.**

Sunset Trail White, vertical box, 6×6×4 inches, **$195.**

Sunset Trail, vertical box, paper label, 6×6×4 inches, **$90.**

Sunset Trail, vertical box, 6×3×3 inches, **$195.**

Sunset Trail Dark Blue, vertical box, 6×6×4 inches, **$195**.

Swell Goods, vertical box, 6×4×4 inches, **$45**.

Sunset Trailers, round, 5×4½ inches, **$350**.

Tentador, horizontal box, paper label, 4×3×1 inches, **$20**.

Tobacco Girl, vertical box, 6×3×3 inches, **$195**.

Tom Keene, vertical box, paper label, 6×4×2 inches, **$15.**

Tom Moore, horizontal box, 5×3½×1 inches, **$20.**

Train Master, vertical box, 6×4×4 inches, **$25.**

Two Belles, horizontal box, 6×4×4 inches, **$25.**

Two Orphans, round, 6×4 inches, **$90.**

Van Loo, vertical box, 5×3×1 inches, **$20.**

Van Bibber, vertical pocket, $4 \times 1\frac{1}{2}$ inches, **$35.**

War Eagle, round, 6×4 inches, **$35.**

Vanko, vertical box, $6 \times 6 \times 4$ inches, **$25.**

War Eagle, round, 5×3 inches, **$35.**

Victor, square flat, $3 \times 3 \times \frac{1}{4}$ inches, **$15.**

WDK, vertical box, $5 \times 2 \times 2$ inches, **$15.**

White Ash, horizontal box, $4 \times 3 \times 1$ inches, **$20.**

Webster, horizontal box, $4 \times 3 \times 1$ inches, **$16.**

Webster Whiffs, horizontal box, $4 \times 3 \times \frac{1}{2}$ inches, **$20.**

Wm. Penn, vertical box, $4 \times 2 \times 2$ inches, **$20.**

Wheeling Maids, round, $6 \times 3\frac{1}{2}$ inches, **$85.**

Winsome, square flat, $3 \times 3 \times \frac{1}{4}$ inches, **$40.**

Y-B, horizontal box, $4 \times 3 \times 1$ inches, **$12.**

Yellow Cab, round, $6 \times 4\frac{1}{2}$ inches, **$225.**

662, round, $5 \times 3\frac{1}{2}$ inches, **$20.**

872, round, 6×3 inches, **$20.**

Pocket Tins

Unless otherwise noted, pocket tobacco tins pictured in this section all feature lithographed tin labels.

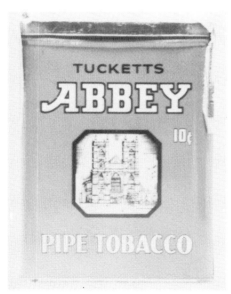

Abbey, 4 × 2½ inches, **$100.**

Aero Club, 3 × 2 inches, **$195.**

Air Ship, cardboard, 3 × 1½ inches, **$400.**

Alumni, 3×2 inches, **$500.**

Bambino, 4×2½ inches, **$800.**

American, 4×2 inches, **$100.**

Barking Dog, paper label, 4×2 inches, **$175.**

Bagdad, 3½×3 inches, **$50.**

Big Ben, 4 × 2 inches, **$500.**

Bluebadge, 4 × 2 inches, **$600.**

Black & White, 4 × 2 inches, **$175.**

Bon-Air, 4 × 2½ inches, **$25.**

Blendwell, 4 × 2 inches, **$90.**

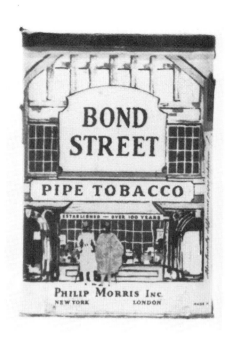

Bond Street, 4 × 2½ inches, **$12.**

Briggs, 4 × 2½ inches, **$12.**

Bowl of Roses, 3 × 2 inches, **$90.**

Buckingham, 4 × 2½ inches, **$40.**

Budweiser, cardboard, $3\frac{1}{2} \times 2\frac{1}{2}$ inches, **$175.**

Canadian Club, 4×2 inches, **$325.**

Bulldog, 3×2 inches, **$100.**

Cannons, $4 \times 2\frac{1}{2}$ inches, **$70.**

Burley Boy, $4 \times 2\frac{1}{2}$ inches, **$500.**

Cardinal, 4×2 inches, **$550.**

Carlton Club, $4 \times 2\frac{1}{2}$ inches, **$85.**

Checkers, $4 \times 2\frac{1}{2}$ inches, **$175.**

Chesapeake, 4×2 inches, **$325.**

Central Union, 4×3 inches, **$65.**

City Club, $4\frac{1}{2} \times 2\frac{1}{2}$ inches, **$75.**

Club Lido, 3 × 2½ inches, **$35.**

Commodore, 3 × 2 inches, **$350.**

Coach and Four, 4 × 2½ inches, **$30.**

Continental Cubes, 3½ × 2½ inches, **$400.**

College Yell, 4½ × 3 inches, **$750.**

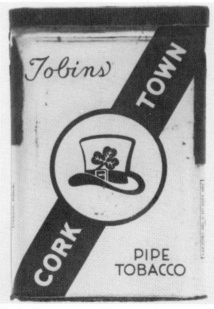

Cork Town, 4 × 2½ inches, **$100.**

Dearstyne's, paper label, $3\frac{1}{2} \times 2$ inches, **$80.**

Culture, $4 \times 2\frac{1}{2}$ inches, **$50.**

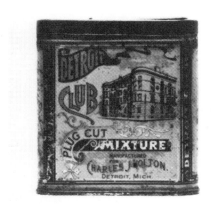

Detroit Club, $4 \times 2\frac{1}{2}$ inches, **$650.**

D & M, paper label, $4 \times 2\frac{1}{2} \times 1\frac{1}{2}$ inches, **$25.**

De Voe's Makings, 4 × 2 inches, **$125.**

Dial, 4 × 2½ inches, **$15.**

De Voe's Sweet Smoke, 4 × 2½ inches,
$125.

Dignity, paper label, 3½ × 2 inches, **$65.**

Dill's Best, 4 × 2 inches, **$25.**

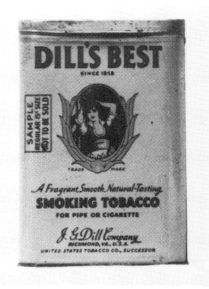

Dill's Best, 4 × 2 inches, **$25.**

Dill's Best, 4 × 2½ inches, **$18.**

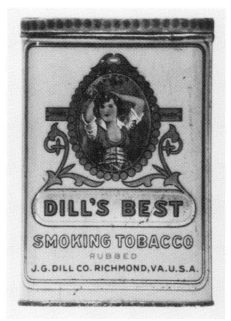

Dill's Best, 4 × 2½ inches, **$15.**

Donniford, paper label, $4 \times 2\frac{1}{2}$ inches, **$25.**

Eden, 3×2 inches, **$150.**

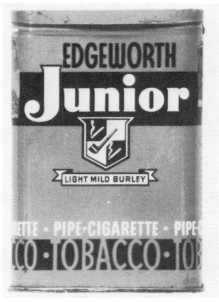

Edgeworth, 4×2 inches, **$15.**

Dunnsboro, $4 \times 2\frac{1}{2}$ inches, **$325.**

English Walnut, 4×2 inches, **$90.**

Ensign, 4 × 2 inches, **$175.**

Epicure, V-corner, 4 × 2½ inches, **$70.**

Essex, 4 × 2 inches, **$1,000 + .**

Epicure, round corners, 4 × 2½ inches,
$150.

Eutopia, 4 × 3 inches, **$175.**

Fairmount, 4 × 2 inches, **$60.**

Eve, 4 × 2½ inches, **$100.**

Falstaff, cardboard, 2 × 1½ inches, **$150.**

F–F, 4 × 2 inches, **$350.**

Fatogo, 4 × 2 inches, **$35.**

Forest & Stream, 4 × 2 inches, **$350.**

Forest & Stream, 4 × 2½ inches, **$50.**

Federation, paper label, 4 × 2 inches, **$35.**

Forest & Stream, 4 × 2 inches, **$75.**

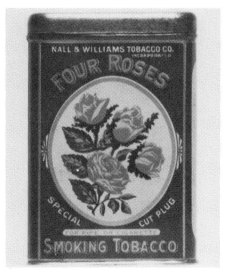

Four Roses, 4 × 2 inches, **$175.**

Four Roses, 4 × 2 inches, **$40.**

Full Dress, 4 × 2 inches, **$275.**

Four Roses, 4 × 2 inches, **$100.**

Full Dress, 4 × 2 inches, **$100.**

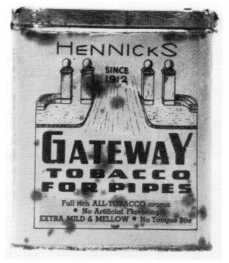

Gateway, paper label, 4 × 2 inches, **$40.**

Gold Shore, 4 × 2 inches, **$175.**

Gibson Girl, 3 × 2 inches, **$100.**

Golden Sceptre, 4 × 2 inches, **$50.**

Gold Dust, 4 × 2 inches, **$1,000 + .**

Golden Sceptre, 4 × 2½ inches, **$50.**

Grain Plug, 3½ × 3 inches, **$25.**

Granulated 54, 4 × 2½ inches, **$55.**

Granger, 4 × 2 inches, **$250.**

Great Blend Flake, 4 × 2½ inches, **$25.**

Granulated 54, paper label, 4 × 2 inches, **$50.**

Guide, 4 × 2 inches, **$125.**

Hand Made, 4 × 2 inches, **$100.**

Half & Half, 4 × 2 inches, **$15.**

Hi-Ho, 4 × 2 inches, **$300.**

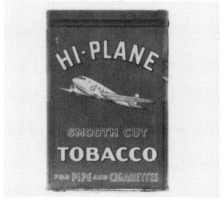

Hi Plane, 4 × 2 inches, **$25.**

Hi Plane, 4 × 2 inches, **$25.**

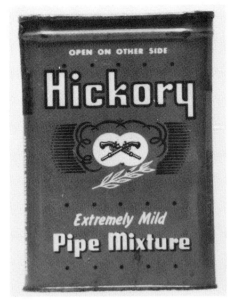

Hickory, 4 × 2½ inches, **$25.**

Hi Plane, 4 × 2 inches, **$100.**

High Grade, 4 × 2½ inches, **$175.**

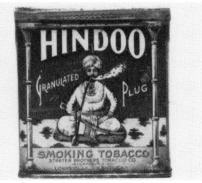

Hindoo, 3 × 2½ inches, **$150.**

Holiday, 4 × 2 inches, **$12.**

Honeymoon, 4 × 2 inches, **$75.**

Honeymoon, 4 × 2 inches, **$75.**

Honeymoon, 4 × 2 inches, **$75.**

Honeymoon, 4 × 2 inches, **$250.**

Hot Scotch, paper label, $3 \times 2\frac{1}{2}$ inches, **$90.**

Howard Kailin's, paper label, 4×2 inches, **$25.**

Hugh Campbell's, 4×2 inches, **$150.**

Hunt Club, $4 \times 2\frac{1}{2}$ inches, **$750.**

Imported & Domestic, paper label, $3\frac{1}{2} \times 2$ inches, **$35.**

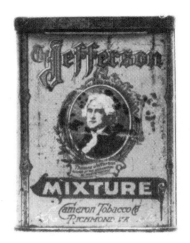

Jefferson, 4 × 2½ inches, **$800.**

Kentucky Club, 4 × 2 inches, **$12.**

John's, paper label, 2½ × 2 inches, **$35.**

Kimbo, cardboard, 4 × 1½ inches, **$60.**

King Edward, 4 × 2½ inches, **$250.**

Life, 4 × 2½ inches, **$100.**

King George, 4 × 2 inches, **$100.**

London Sherbet, 4 × 2½ inches, **$40.**

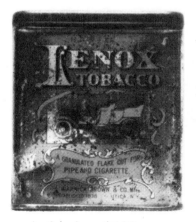

Lenox, 4 × 2 inches, **$400.**

London Sherbet, 4 × 2 inches, **$35.**

Louisiana Perique, paper label, 4 × 2 inches, **$125.**

Look Out, 4 × 2½ inches, **$300.**

Loving Cup, 4 × 2 inches, **$450.**

Lucky Star, 4 × 2 inches, **$100.**

Lucky Strike, 3 × 1½ inches, **$40.**

Lucky Strike, 4 × 2 inches, **$200.**

Luxura, 3½ × 2 inches, **$200.**

Lucky Strike, 4 × 2½ inches, **$35.**

Manco, 4 × 2 inches, **$175.**

Manhattan Cocktail, 4×2 inches, **$90.**

Maryland Club, 3½×3 inches, **$250.**

Mariposa, 3×2½ inches, **$190.**

Maryland Club, 4×2 inches, **$100.**

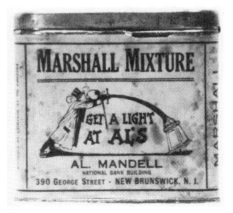

Marshall Mixture, paper label, 3×2 inches, **$40.**

Master Mason, 4×2 inches, **$850.**

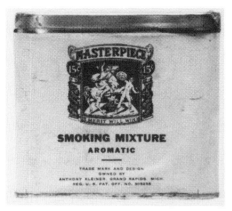

Masterpiece, paper label, 3 × 2½ inches, **$25.**

Matoaka, 4 × 2 inches, **$375.**

Meerschaum, cardboard, 3 × 2½ inches, **$350.**

Model, 4 × 2 inches, **$14.**

Moonshine, 4 × 2 inches, **$250.**

Old Colony, 4 × 2 inches, **$75.**

Old Squire, 4 × 2 inches, **$200.**

Old Virginia, 4 × 2 inches, **$200.**

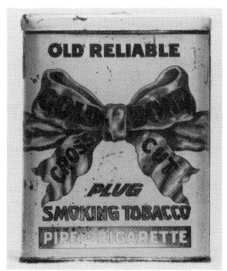

Old Reliable, 3 × 2 inches, **$75.**

Our Own, paper label, 4 × 2 inches, **$40.**

Pat Hand, 2 × 2 inches, **$45.**

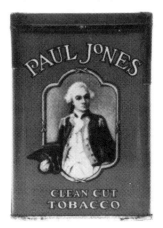

Paul Jones, 4 × 2½ inches, **$500.**

Palmy Days, 4 × 2 inches, **$100.**

Peachey, 3½ × 2 inches, **$50.**

Penn's No. 1, 4 × 2 inches, **$300.**

Picobac, 4 × 2 and 3½ × 2 inches, **$30.**

Pinkussohn's, 3 × 2½ inches, **$45.**

Pinkussohn's, paper label, 3 × 2½ inches, **$20.**

Pipe Major, 4 × 2 inches, **$225.**

Pony Express, paper label, 4×2 inches, **$45.**

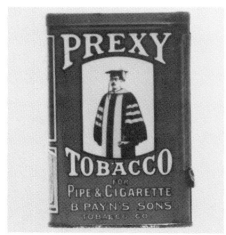

Prexy (Yellow Stripes), 4×2 inches, **$750.**

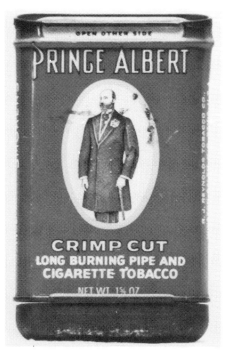

Prince Albert, 4×2 inches, **$12.**

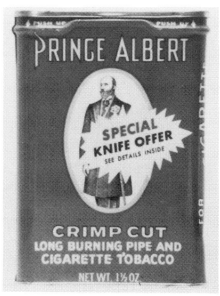

Prince Albert, 4×2 inches, **$12.**

Puritan, 4×2 inches, **$90.**

Q Boid, 4×2 inches, **$35.**

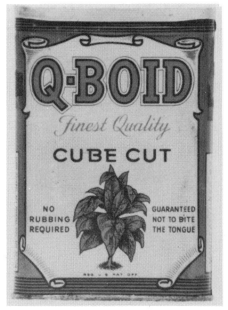

Q Boid, 4×2 inches, **$25.**

Queed, 4×2 inches, **$45.**

Red Belt, 3 × 1½ inches, **$25.**

Red and Blue, 4 × 2 inches, **$375.**

Red Jacket, 4 × 2½ inches, **$25.**

Regal, 4 × 2½ inches, **$95.**

Reposed, 4 × 2 inches, **$190.**

Revelation, 4×2 and 3½×2½ inches, **$12.**

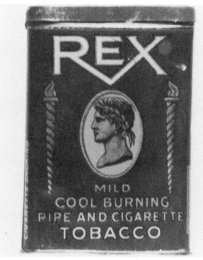

Rochester Club, 4×2 inches, **$200.**

Rex, 4×2½ inches, **$50.**

Rock Castle, 3½×2½ inches, **$450.**

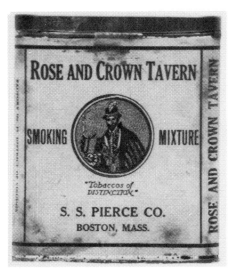

Rose & Crown Tavern, paper label, 3½ × 2 inches, **$200.**

Rose Leaf, 3½ × 1½ inches, **$75.**

Rothenberg's, 3 × 2½ inches, **$100.**

Schermerhorn's, paper label, 3 × 3 inches, **$12.**

Schermerhorn's, paper label, 4 × 2 inches, **$12.**

Schulte's, paper label, 4 × 2 inches, **$40.**

Shot Crushed, 4 × 2 inches, **$25.**

Scissors, 4 × 2 inches, **$750.**

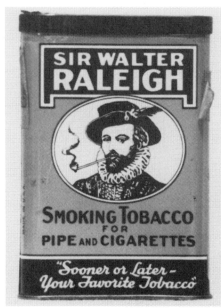

Sir Walter Raleigh, 4 × 2 inches, **$12.**

Smoke Shop, paper label, 4 × 2½ inches, **$40.**

Snyder's 331, paper label, 4 × 2 inches, **$85.**

Snap Shots, 4 × 2½ inches, **$200.**

Stag, 4 × 2 inches, **$30.**

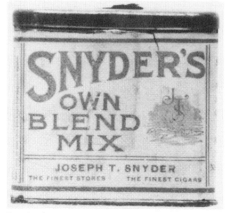

Snyder's, paper label, 3½ × 2 inches, **$40.**

Stanwix, 4 × 2 inches, **$190.**

Star, 2½ × 1½ inches, **$25.**

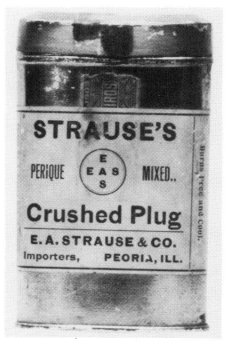

Strause's, paper label, 3½ × 2 inches, **$40.**

Sun Cured, 4 × 2½ inches, **$425.**

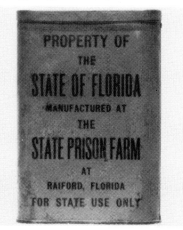

State of Florida, 4 × 2 inches, **$25.**

Sun Cured, paper label, $4 \times 2\frac{1}{2}$ inches, **$225.**

Sweet Violet, $4 \times 2\frac{1}{2}$ inches, **$350.**

T&B (Freeport, Il.), 3×2 inches, **$175.**

Sweet Tips, paper label, $3\frac{1}{2} \times 2$ inches, **$30.**

Taxi, 4×2 inches, **$1,000 +.**

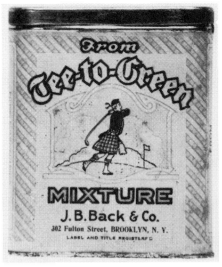

Tee to Green, paper label, $4 \times 3\frac{1}{2}$ inches, **$85.**

Times Square, $4 \times 2\frac{1}{2}$ inches, **$175.**

Three Feathers, 4×2 inches, **$100.**

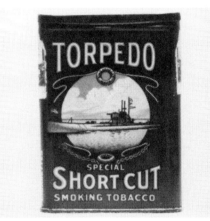

Torpedo, 4×2 inches, **$900.**

Totem, $3 \times 1\frac{1}{2}$ inches, **$450.**

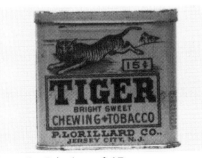

Tiger, 3×3 inches, **$45.**

95

Trout Line, 3 × 2 inches, **$325.**

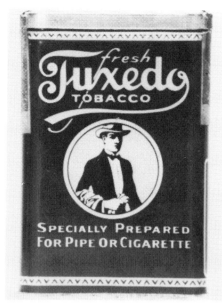

Tuxedo, 4 × 2 inches, **$12.**

Turkish Patrol, 4 × 2 inches, **$100.**

Twin Oaks, 4 × 2 inches, **$90.**

Tuxedo, 4 × 2½ inches, **$20.**

Twin Oaks, 4 × 2 inches, **40.**

Ty Cobb, 4 × 2 inches, **$1,000 + .**

Union Leader, 4 × 2 inches, **$30.**

U.S. Marine, 4 × 2 inches, **$100.**

Union Leader, 4 × 2 inches, **$30.**

Uncle Sam, 4 × 2 inches, **$1,000 + .**

Union Leader, 4 × 2 inches, **$30.**

Unity, 2×1½ inches, **$200.**

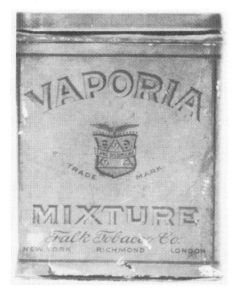

Vaporia, paper label, 4×3 inches, **$25.**

Velvet, 3×2 inches, **$14.**

Velvet, 4×2 inches, **$12.**

Wagon Wheel, 4×2 inches, **$200.**

98

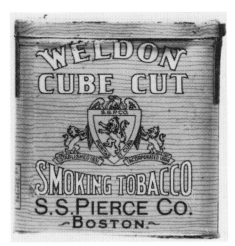

Weldon, 3×2 inches, **$30.**

Wellington, 4×2 inches, **$85.**

Whip, 4×2 and 3½×2 inches, **$325.**

White Manor, 3×2 inches, **$90.**

Wild Fruit, 4×2 inches, **$325.**

Willoughby Taylor, 4×2 inches, **$30.**

Yacht Club, 4 × 2 inches, **$250.**

Ye Olde Blende, paper label, 4 × 2½ inches, **$80.**

Yankee Boy, 3 × 2½ inches, **$300.**

54, 4 × 2 inches, **$30.**

Buckingham, sample tin, **$50.**

Half & Half, sample tin, **$60.**

Edgeworth, sample tin, **$35.**

Edgeworth, sample tin, **$45.**

Hi Plane, sample tin, **$60.**

Full Dress, sample tin, **$85.**

Old Colony, sample tin, **$85.**

Revelation, sample tin, **$30.**

Granulated 54, sample tin, **$60.**

Sir Walter Raleigh, sample tin, **$25.**

Union Leader, sample tin, **$40.**

Sweet Tips, sample tin, **$50.**

Velvet, sample tin, **$50.**

Velvet, sample tin, **$40.**

Twin Oaks, sample tin, **$60.**

Tobacco Pails

Unless otherwise noted, the tobacco pails pictured in this section are bail-handled and feature lithographed tin labels.

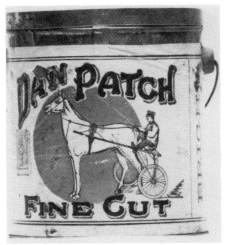

Dan Patch, paper label, 8 × 5 inches, **$65.**

Dan Patch, paper label, 18 × 8 × 20 inches, **$100.**

Fast Mail, 5 × 4 × 3 inches, **$800.**

Frishmuth's, 7×5 inches, **$50.**

Golden Thread, paper label, 5×6 inches, **$50.**

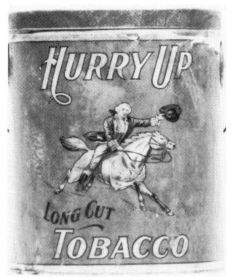

Hurry Up, paper label, 7×5 inches, **$175.**

Magnet, 6×3½ inches, **$375.**

May Flower, 6×5×4 inches, **$600.**

Ojibwa, 7×5 inches, **$225.**

Miners & Puddlers, 7×5 inches, **$100.**

Old Partner, 7×5 inches, **$100.**

Nigger Hair, 7×5 inches, **$110.**

Old Rover, 7×5 inches, **$100.**

Seven Up, 7×5 inches, **$225.**

Penns, 7×5 inches, **$30.**

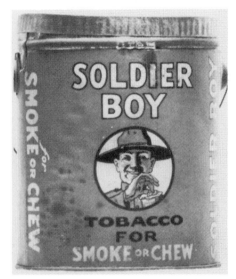

Soldier Boy, paper label, 7×5 inches, **$100.**

Sweet Mist, 7×4 inches, **$60.**

Virgin, paper label, 2½ × 2½ inches, **$1,000 +**.

Lunch Box Tins

Unless otherwise noted, all of the lunch box tins pictured in this section feature lithographed tin labels.

Arrow, paper label, 7×4×3 inches, **$80.**

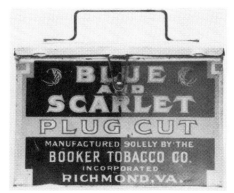
Blue & Scarlet, 6×4×4 inches, **$400.**

Brotherhood, 6×5×4 inches, **$35.**

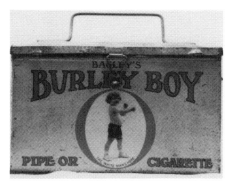

Burley Boy, 5×4½×4 inches, **$800.**

Central Union, 5×6×3½ inches, **$35.**

Buzz, paper label, 6×5×4 inches, **$90.**

Central Union, 8×6×4 inches, **$45.**

Comet, paper label, 7×4×3 inches, **$90.**

Country Club, 6×4×4 inches, **$400.**

Cub, paper label, 6×5×3½ inches, **$40.**

Dixie Kid, black, 6×5×4 inches, **$250.**

Dixie Kid, white, 6×5×4 inches, **$250.**

Dixie Queen, 6×5×4 inches, **$100.**

Fashion, 6×5×4 inches, **$50.**

Friends, 6×5×4 inches, **$100.**

Friends, paper label, 6×4½ inches, **$90.**

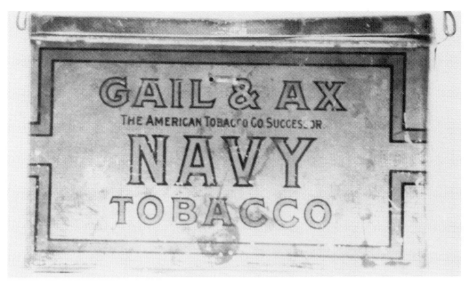

Gail & Ax, 6×5×4 inches, **$50.**

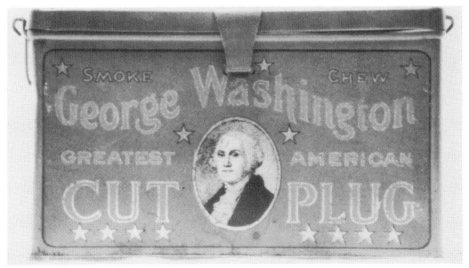

George Washington, 6×5×4 inches, **$30.**

George Washington, 6×4×3 inches, **$20.**

Gold Shore, 5×4½×4 inches, **$95.**

Handbag, irregular shape, **$65.**

H-O, 5×4½×3 inches, **$50.**

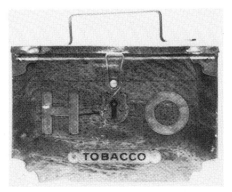

Just Suits, 6×5×4 inches, **$35.**

King Koal, 6×5×4 inches, **$45.**

Laredo, 5×4×3 inches, **$40.**

Lorillard's Stripped, 10×7×6 inches, **$35.**

Lucky Curve, 4×6×5 inches, **$250.**

Main Brace, 5×4×3 inches, **$30.**

Mastiff, $7 \times 4\frac{1}{2} \times 4\frac{1}{2}$ inches, **$800.**

Mayos, $7 \times 6 \times 4$ inches, **$100.**

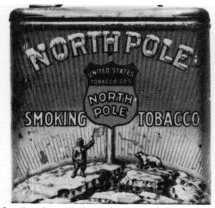

Pedro, $6 \times 5 \times 4$ inches, **$75.**

Northpole, $4 \times 6 \times 3$ inches, **$65.**

Penny Post, 6×5×4 inches, **$100.**

Penny Post, 6×5×4 inches, **$100.**

Plow Boy, 6×5×4 inches, **$250.**

Rainbow, 7×5×3 inches, **$300.**

Red Crown, 6×5×4½ inches, **$45.**

Red Indian, 6×5×4 inches, **$400.**

Red Indian, 6×5×4 inches, **$800.**

Round Trip, 6×4×4 inches, **$125.**

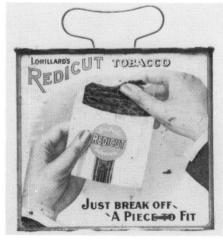

Redicut, 6×6×2½ inches, **$100.**

Satisfaction, 7×5×3 inches, **$95.**

Sensation, irregular shape, **$100.**

Sensation, 6×5×4 inches, **$35.**

Tiger, 8×6×6 inches, **$35.**

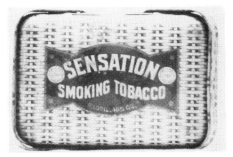

Sweet Cuba, 6×5×2½ inches, **$30.**

Union Commander, 7×4×4 inches, **$250.**

Union Leader, 6×5×4 inches, **$35.**   Union Leader, 6×5×4 inches, **$25.**

U.S. Marine, 6×5×4 inches, **$275.**

Warnick & Brown, 6×5×4 inches, **$50.**   Winner, 6×5×4 inches, **$90.**

Winner, 7×5×4 inches, **$90.**

Roly Polys

All of the roly poly tins pictured in this section have lithographed tin labels. They measure approximately 7 inches in height.

Satisfied Customer, **$450.**

Storekeeper, **$400.**

Singing Waiter, **$400.**

The Dutchman, **$450.**

Mammy, **$400.**

Inspector (Man from Scotland Yard), **$700.**

Cigarette Tins

All of the cigarette tins pictured in this section have lithographed tin labels.

After Lunch, square flat, $3 \times 3 \times \frac{1}{4}$ inches, **$25.**

After Lunch, square flat, $3 \times 3 \times \frac{1}{4}$ inches, **$25.**

Alumni, square flat, $3 \times 3 \times \frac{1}{4}$ inches, **$20.**

ATCO, square flat, $3 \times 3 \times \frac{1}{4}$ inches, **$20.**

122

Beatall, square flat, $3 \times 2\frac{1}{2} \times \frac{1}{4}$ inches, **$20.**

Bounty, pack, $2\frac{1}{2} \times 2$ inches, **$12.**

Camel, flat 50, $6 \times 4 \times \frac{1}{4}$ inches, **$25.**

Camel, round, $3 \times 2\frac{1}{2}$ inches, **$30.**

Casino, flat 50, $6 \times 4 \times \frac{1}{4}$ inches, **$30.**

Cavalier, oval, 4×3 inches, **$10.**

Chesterfield, flat 50, 6×4×¼ inches, **$10.**

Coronation, flat 50, 6×4×¼ inches, **$15.**

Coronation, flat 50, 6×4×¼ inches, **$12.**

Coronation, flat 50, 6×4×¼ inches, **$15.**

Darling, square flat, 3×3×¼ inches, **$25.**

Dimitrino, horizontal box, 6×4×1½ inches, **$25.**

Dixie, flat 50, 6×4×½ inches, **$50.**

Egyptian Belles, square flat, $3 \times 3 \times \frac{1}{4}$ inches, **$35.**

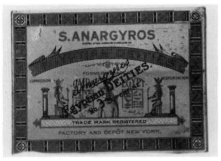

Egyptian Deities, flat 100, $6 \times 4 \times \frac{1}{2}$ inches, **$25.**

Egyptian Delight, flat 50, $6 \times 4 \times \frac{1}{4}$ inches, **$25.**

Embassy, pack, $4 \times 2\frac{1}{2}$ inches, **$15.**

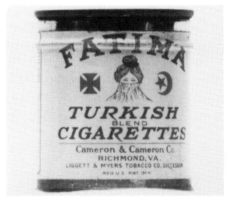

Fatima, round, $3 \times 1\frac{1}{2}$ inches, **$30.**

Fatima, flat 50, $6 \times 4 \times \frac{1}{2}$ inches, **$25.**

Gaiety Girl, square flat, $3 \times 3 \times \frac{1}{4}$ inches, **$90.**

Helmar, flat 50, $6 \times 4 \times \frac{1}{2}$ inches, **$20.**

Gold Flake, horizontal box, $10 \times 5 \times 4$ inches, **$20.**

Herbert Tareyton, flat 100, $6 \times 3\frac{1}{2} \times 1$ inches, **$15.**

Great Auk, horizontal box, $6 \times 2\frac{1}{2} \times 1\frac{1}{2}$ inches, **$400.**

Herbert Tareyton, round, $2\frac{1}{2} \times 1\frac{1}{2}$ inches, **$15.**

Handsome Dan, square flat, $3 \times 3 \times \frac{1}{4}$ inches, **$95.**

Kentucky Winners, flat 50, $6 \times 4 \times \frac{1}{2}$ inches, **$35.**

Kool, flat 50, $6 \times 4 \times \frac{1}{4}$ inches, **$35.**

Lucky Strike, flat 50, $6 \times 4 \times \frac{1}{4}$ inches, **$13.**

Lucky Strike, flat 50, $6 \times 4 \times \frac{1}{4}$ inches, **$13.**

Lucky Strike, flat 50, $6 \times 4 \times \frac{1}{4}$ inches, **$40.**

Lucky Strike, flat 50, $6 \times 4 \times \frac{1}{4}$ inches, **$25.**

Lucky Strike, pack, $2\frac{1}{2} \times 2\frac{1}{2}$ inches, **$100.**

Mah Mal, vertical box, 5×2×1 inches, **$15.**

Marlboro, round, 3×1½ inches, **$25.**

Marlboro, round, 3×1½ inches, **$30.**

Marlboro, flat 50, 6×4×¼ inches, **$15.**

Melachrino, flat 100, 6×4×½ inches, **$15.**

Murad, flat 50, 6×4×¼ inches, **$15.**

Murad, pack, $2 \times 2\frac{1}{2}$ inches, **$25.**

Nestor, horizontal box, $3 \times 2 \times \frac{1}{2}$ inches, **$25.**

Nizam, horizontal box, $3 \times 2 \times \frac{1}{4}$ inches, **$25.**

Old Gold, pack, 4×2 inches, **$20.**

Old Gold, flat 50, $6 \times 4 \times \frac{1}{4}$ inches, **$25.**

Omar, flat 50, $6 \times 4 \times \frac{1}{4}$ inches, **$12.**

Pall Mall, horizontal box, $4 \times 2 \times 1$ inches, **$15.**

Philip Morris, pack, $4 \times 2 \times 1$ inches, **$10.**

Pall Mall, horizontal box, $8 \times 6 \times 2$ inches, **$25.**

Player's, flat 50, $6 \times 4 \times \frac{1}{2}$ inches, **$12.**

Pall Mall, horizontal box, $8 \times 6 \times 2$ inches, **$30.**

Player's No. 3, flat 50, $6 \times 4 \times \frac{1}{2}$ inches, **$12.**

Passing Show, flat 50, $6 \times 4 \times \frac{1}{2}$ inches, **$20.**

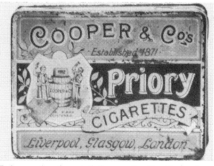

Priory, horizontal box, $4 \times 3 \times 1$ inches, **$30.**

Regelo, horizontal box, $3 \times 2\frac{1}{2} \times \frac{1}{2}$ inches, **$12.**

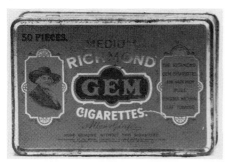

Richmond Gem, horizontal box, $3 \times 2\frac{1}{2} \times \frac{1}{2}$ inches, **$12.**

Sarony, flat 100, $6 \times 4 \times \frac{1}{2}$ inches, **$25.**

Shirley, square flat, $3 \times 3 \times \frac{1}{4}$ inches, **$25.**

Smiles, flat 50, $6 \times 4 \times \frac{1}{4}$ inches, **$50.**

Snake Charmer, vertical box, $6 \times 2 \times 1$ inches, **$50.**

Sportsman, flat 50, 6 × 4 × ¼ inches, **$12.**

Weekend, oval, 2½ × 2½ inches, **$100.**

Sullivan, Powell, horizontal box, 5 × 2 × 2 inches, **$15.**

White Star Line, horizontal box, 4 × 2½ × ½ inches, **$45.**

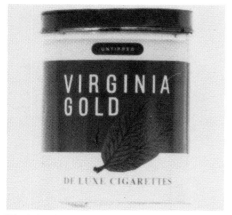

Virginia Gold, round, 3 × 2 inches, **$12.**

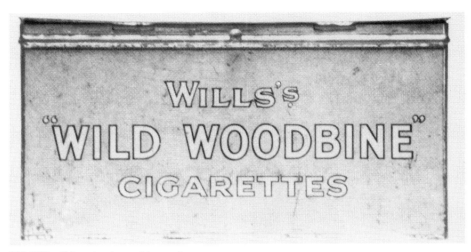

Wild Woodbine, horizontal box, size uncertain, **$75.**

Winning Team, horizontal box, $3 \times 2 \times 1$ inches, **$200.**

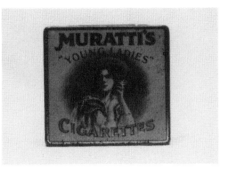

Young Ladies, square flat, $3 \times 3 \times \frac{1}{4}$ inches, **$90.**

Cylindrical Containers

Unless otherwise noted, all of the cylindrical containers pictured in this section have lithographed tin labels.

Admiral, 6 × 3½ inches, **$50.**

Amber, 4 × 3 inches, **$15.**

Archer, 4 × 3 inches, **$10.**

Bingo, 5 × 4 inches, **$100.**

Big Ben, 6 × 5 inches, **$25.**

Blue Boar, paper label, 2½ × 1¾ inches, **$15.**

Big Hit, paper label, 6 × 5 inches, **$50.**

Blue Boar, paper label, 5 × 3 inches, **$25.**

135

Bond Street, 6×4½ inches, **$14.**

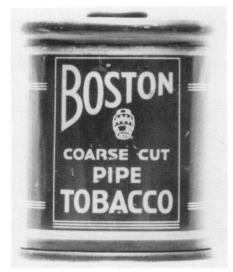

Boston, 6×3 inches, **$30.**

Briggs, 6×4½ inches, **$12.**

Brotherhood, 6×4 inches, **$65.**

Brother Jonathan, 18×12 inches, **$1,500+.**

Bulldog, paper label, 6×5 inches, **$225.**

Brown Bear, paper label, 5×4 inches, **$40.**

Cadillac, 2×8 inches, **$750.**

Buckingham, 6×5 inches, **$30.**

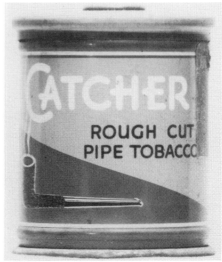

Buckingham, 6×5 inches, **$35.**

Catcher, 6×3 inches, **$30.**

137

Central Union, 6×3 inches, **$50.**

Columbia, 6×3 inches, **$50.**

Chicago Cubs, 3×6 inches, **$25.**

Compass, 4×3 inches, **$50.**

Corn Bread, paper label, 3½×5 inches, **$90.**

City Club, 6×3 inches, **$100.**

Country Life, 4 × 2½ inches, **$25.**

Culture, 6 × 3 inches, **$50.**

Country Life, paper label, 3 × 2 inches, **$25.**

Daily Mail, 5 × 3 inches, **$25.**

Cranes Private, 5 × 3 inches, **$25.**

Dixie Queen, 5 × 3 inches, **$200.**

Dixie Queen, 6 × 3 inches, **$140.**

Edgeworth, 6 × 4 inches, **$12.**

Eight Brothers, 6 × 3 inches, **$25.**

Eskimo, 5½ × 3 inches, **$200.**

Flycasters, 3½ × 4 inches, **$60.**

Fast Mail, cardboard, 14 × 8 inches, **$1,000 +.**

Forest Giant, cardboard, 4 × 4 inches, **$350.**

Fast Mail, paper label, 5 × 3½ inches, **$750.**

Forest & Stream, 5×3 inches, **$80.**

Forest & Stream, 3×2½ inches, **L—$75. R—$275.**

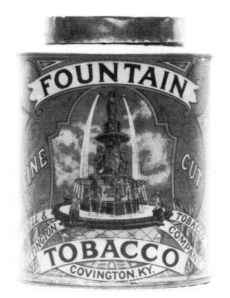

Fountain, 6×3 inches, **$800.**

Game, paper label, 5×4 inches, **$750.**

Fountain, 7×4 inches, **$100.**

George Washington, 6×4 inches, **$12.**

Gold Leaf, paper label, 6×4½ inches, **$100.**

Green River, paper label, 12×12×12 inches, **$45.**

Half & Half, 6×4½ inches, **$14.**

Hand Made, 4×3 inches, **$90.**

Grizzly, paper label, 6×4 inches, **$100.**

144   Hand Made, 6×3 inches, **$100.**

Hardaport, 6×3 inches, **$800.**

H-O, 6×3 inches, **$45.**

Hi Plane, 6×3 inches, **$35.**

Hurley Burley, 6×3 inches, **$30.**

Imperial Cube Cut, 3×1½ inches, **$10.**

Keg, 6×3 inches, **$30.**

Juggler, Ogden's, 6×5 inches, **$35.**

Kite, paper label, 3×5 inches, **$40.**

Lee Camp, cardboard, 4×3 inches, **$350.**

Just Suits, 7×4 inches, **$60.**

Longbottom, paper label, 3 × 2 inches, **$25.**

Magpie, 1 × 2½ inches, **$10.**

Luxury, 6 × 4½ inches, **$20.**

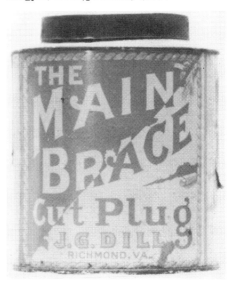

Main Brace, 5 × 3 inches, **$90.**

Mac Donald's Pilot, 5 × 3 inches, **$20.**

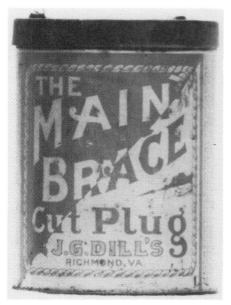

Main Brace, 6×3 inches, **$35.**

Mayo's, paper label, 6×4 inches, **$50.**

Masterpiece, paper label, 4×4 inches, **$15.**

Mellow Sweet, 14×8 inches, **$800.**

Mountie, 2×5 inches, **$30.**

Nic Nac, 14×8 inches, **$850.**

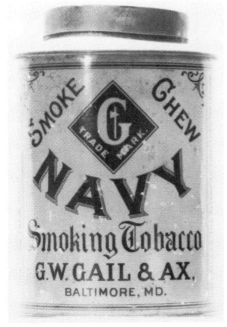

Navy, 6×4 inches, **$125.**

Ojibwa, 14×8 inches, **$225.**

Omar, 2×8 inches, **$40.**

Pedro, 6×3 inches, **$300.**

Omega, 5×3 inches, **$45.**

Pilot, 6×5 inches, **$50.**

Pilot, 5×5 inches, **$90.**

Beer

Pale Ale

Amber

Glass Pilsner

X

Plaza, 5×4 inches, **$100.**

Puritan, cardboard, 3½×3 inches, **$85.**

Plow Boy, paper label, 6×4½ inches, **$12.**

Red Indian, 6×4 inches, **$450.**

Polar, 2½ × 2½ inches, **$400.**

Reposed, 3×3 inches, **$50.**

Seal of North Carolina, 6×3½ inches, **$100.**

Seal of North Carolina, 6×4 inches, **$400.**

Sensation, 6×5 inches, **$25.**

Spugs, 6×3 inches, **$35.**

Sterling, 12×15 inches, **$75.**

Sterling, 14×8 inches, **$40.**

Sterling, 14×8 inches, **$65.**

Sun Cured, 6 × 3½ inches, **$225.**

Sweet Burley, 14 × 8 inches, **$50.**

Sweet Burley, 14 × 8 inches, **$50.**

Sweet Cuba, 14 × 8 inches, **$50.**

Sweet Mist, 14×8 inches, **$60.**

Sweet Mist, 14×8 inches, **$100.**

Target, 4×3 inches, **$10.**

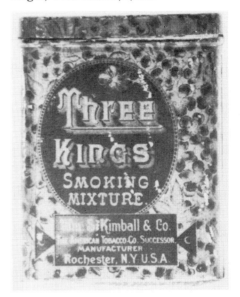

Three Kings, paper label, 3×3 inches, **$25.**

Three Squires, paper label, 3×4 inches, **$12.**

Three States, paper label, 6 × 3 inches, **$350.**

Times Square, paper label, 6 × 4½ inches, **$35.**

Tuxedo, 6 × 3 inches, **$25.**

Tiger, 14 × 8 inches, **$75.**

Tweed, 5 × 5 inches, **$12.**

Twenty Grand, 3×2½ inches, **$25.**

Twin Oaks, paper label, 1½×3 inches, **$75.**

Uniform, 6×3 inches, **$400.**

Union Jack, 5×5 inches, **$50.**

Union Leader, 6×3 inches, **$35.**

Union Leader, 6×3½ inches, **$35.**

Union World, 6×3 inches, **$50.**

Union Leader, 7×3 inches, **$200.**

U.S. Marine, 6×3 inches, **$225.**

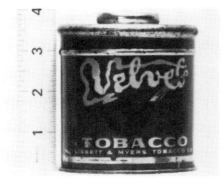

Velvet, 3½ × 3½ inches, **$50.**

White Seal, 6 × 3½ inches, **$25.**

Wellington, 7 × 5 inches, **$12.**

Wild Fruit, 4 × 4 inches, **$25.**

Winner, 6×3 inches, **$100**

Winner, 6×3 inches, **$100**

Miscellaneous Tobacco Containers

Unless otherwise noted, all of the miscellaneous tobacco containers pictured in this section feature lithographed tin labels.

Acme Extra Mild, horizontal box, 6 × 4 × 1 inches, **$25.**

Ace High, horizontal box, $4 \times 1\frac{1}{2} \times \frac{1}{2}$ inches, **$200.**

All Nations, horizontal box, $4 \times 2 \times 1\frac{1}{2}$ inches, **$45.**

Aleppo Temple, horizontal box, $2 \times 1\frac{1}{2} \times \frac{1}{2}$ inches, **$50.**

Alumni, horizontal box, $5 \times 3 \times 3$ inches, **$25.**

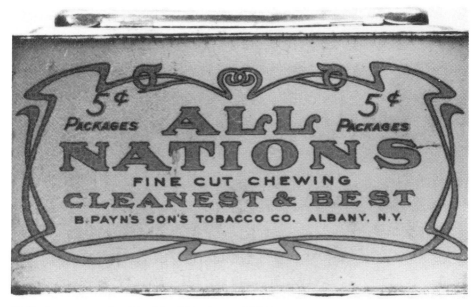

All Nations, store tin, $24 \times 10 \times 12$ inches, **$125.**

American Beauty, horizontal box, $4 \times 2 \times 1$ inches, **$20.**

American Eagle, horizontal box, $5 \times 3 \times 2$ inches, **$100.**

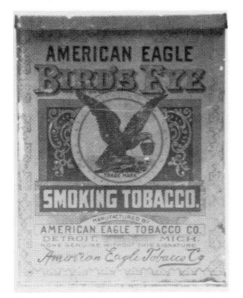

American Eagle, vertical box, $5 \times 3 \times 1$ inches, **$45.**

American Line, horizontal box, $3 \times 2 \times 1\frac{1}{2}$ inches, **$25.**

American Girl, horizontal box, $4 \times 2 \times \frac{1}{2}$ inches, **$350.**

163

American Navy, horizontal box, 6×4×3 inches, **$45.**

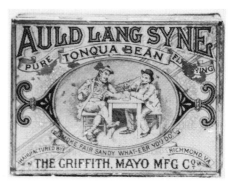

Auld Lang Syne, horizontal box, 3×2×2 inches, **$150.**

Arcadia, horizontal box, 3×3×1 inches, **$20.**

Arcadia Mixture, horizontal box, 5×5×5 inches, **$25.**

Autobacco, vertical box, $4 \times 2\frac{1}{2} \times 1\frac{1}{2}$ inches, **$50.**

Autobacco, horizontal box, 6×4×2 inches, **$50.**

B.F. Gravely's, vertical box, paper label, $6 \times 3\frac{1}{2} \times 2\frac{1}{2}$ inches, **$45.**

Bamboo, square flat, $3 \times 3 \times \frac{3}{4}$ inches, **$25.**

Banner Fine Cut, horizontal box, $3 \times 1\frac{1}{2} \times \frac{1}{2}$ inches, **$350.**

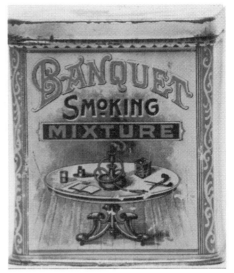

Banquet, vertical box, $3 \times 2 \times 2$ inches, **$50.**

Bat, horizontal box, $3 \times 2 \times 2$ inches, **$50.**

Belfast, vertical box, $7 \times 6 \times 3$ inches, **$18.**

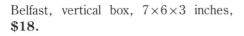

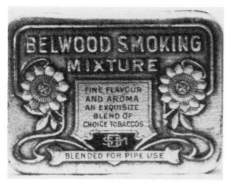

Belwood, horizontal box, 3 × 2 × 1 inches, **$20**.

Best, horizontal box, paper label, 6 × 6 × 4 inches, **$100**.

Berta Gravely, vertical box, 4 × 3 × 2 inches, **$1,000 +** .

Blue Label, horizontal box, 4 × 2 × 1 inches, **$40**.

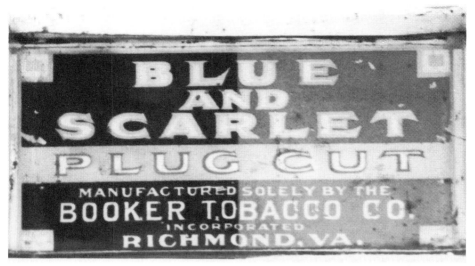

Blue & Scarlet, horizontal box, 4×6×3 inches, **$50.**

Boar's Head, horizontal box, 8×5×5 inches, **$50.**

Bob White, vertical box, 5×4×2 inches, **$200.**

Bob White, horizontal box, 3×2½×1½ inches, **$200.**

Bohemian, horizontal box, 4×4×4 inches, **$1,000+**.

Boston Slice, horizontal box, 6×4×3 inches, **$100.**

Boston Slice, horizontal box, 4×3×1 inches, **$45.**

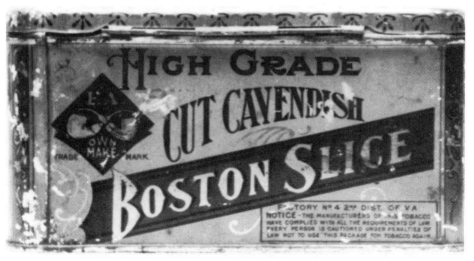

Boston Slice, horizontal box, 4×3×1 inches, **$45.**

Brandon Mixture, horizontal box, $3 \times 1 \times 2\frac{1}{2}$ inches, **$25.**

Brilliant Mixture, horizontal box, $4 \times 2 \times 1$ inches, **$40.**

Brilliant Mixture, horizontal box, $3 \times 2 \times 1\frac{1}{2}$ inches, **$40.**

Brotherhood, horizontal box, 6×4×3 inches, **$25.**

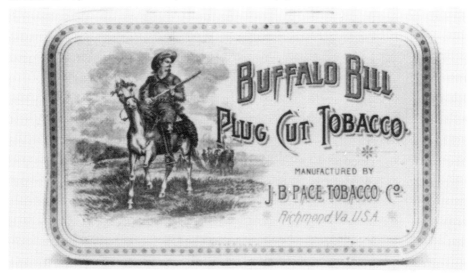

Buffalo Bill, horizontal box, 6×4×2 inches, **$225.**

Bulldog Brand, horizontal box, 4×3×1 inches, **$15.**

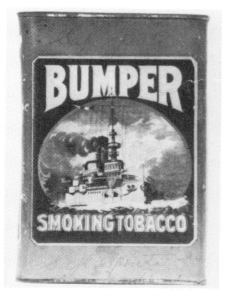

Bumper, vertical box, cardboard, 6×4×4 inches, **$50.**

Bushranger, horizontal box, 4×3×1 inches, **$20.**

Cake Box, horizontal box, 4×3×2 inches, **$20.**

Cake Box, horizontal box, 6×4×3 inches, **$15.**

Calabash, flat-round, 2×3 inches, **$20.**

Calabash, horizontal box, 4×3×1 inches, **$20.**

California Nugget, oval, 3×2 inches, **$100.**

Cambridge Mixture, horizontal box, 4×3×2 inches, **$75.**

California Nugget, horizontal box, 4×2½×½ inches, **$50.**

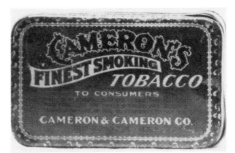

Cameron's, horizontal box, 4×6×2 inches, **$50.**

Cameron's, horizontal box, 4×6×2 inches, **$50.**

Cameron's Pocket Slice, square flat, $3 \times 3 \times \frac{1}{2}$ inches, **$20.**

Cameron's Finest Grade, horizontal box, $6 \times 5 \times 4$ inches, **$100.**

Cameron's Finest Grade, horizontal box, $6 \times 5 \times 4$ inches, **$100.**

Cameron's Finest Grade, horizontal box, $6 \times 5 \times 4$ inches, **$100.**

Cameron's Finest Grade, horizontal box, $6 \times 5 \times 4$ inches, **$100.**

Canuck, horizontal box, $4 \times 3 \times 1\frac{1}{2}$ inches, **$20.**

Carnation, horizontal box, 4 × 3 × 2 inches, **$85.**

Catac Mixture, horizontal box, 3 × 2 × 1 inches, **$40.**

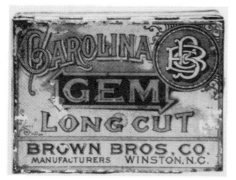

Carolina Gem, horizontal box, 3 × 2 × 2 inches, **$45.**

Cavalier, horizontal box, 4 × 3 × 1 inches, **$40.**

Catac Mixture, horizontal box, 3 × 2 × 2 inches, **$40.**

174

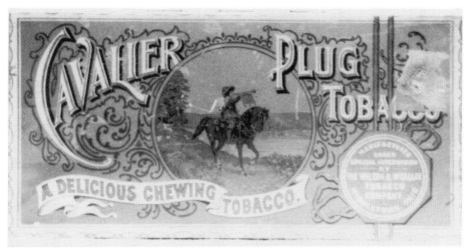

Cavalier, horizontal box, 6×3×1 inches, **$75.**

Central Union, horizontal box, 6×4×3 inches, **$22.**

Century, horizontal box, 3×1×½ inches, **$75.**

Century, horizontal box, 3×1×½ inches, **$75.**

C.H.Y.P., horizontal box, 4 × 3 × 2 inches, **$225.**

Charm of the West, horizontal box, 3½ × 1½ × ½ inches, **$400.**

Challenge Flake, horizontal box, 4 × 3 × 1 inches, **$25.**

Checkers, oval, 5 × 4 × 3 inches, **$200.**

Champagne, vertical box, 3 × 1 × 3 inches, **$30.**

Chicago Club, horizontal box, 3½ × 2½ × 1½ inches, **$15.**

Cleveland Centennial, horizontal box, 5×3×2 inches, **$225.**

Columbia Dome, horizontal box, 3×2×1 inches, **$600.**

Continental Cubes, horizontal box, 5×5×5 inches, **$450.**

Constellation, horizontal box, 4×3×1 inches, **$25.**

Control, horizontal box, 4×3×2 inches, **$200.**

Cornell, vertical box, 4×2×1 inches, **$50.**

Cosmos, horizontal box, 4×3×2 inches, **$90.**

Country Life, horizontal box, 4×3×1 inches, **$25.**

Creole, vertical box, 5×3×2 inches, **$200.**

Crescent Club, horizontal box, 4×3×2 inches, **$45.**

Critic, horizontal box, $3\frac{1}{2} \times 1\frac{1}{2} \times 1\frac{1}{2}$ inches, **$20.**

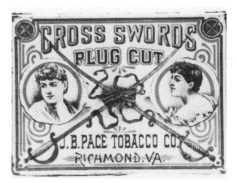

Cross Swords, horizontal box, $4 \times 3 \times 1$ inches, **$50.**

Cupid, square flat, $3 \times 3 \times \frac{1}{2}$ inches, **$45.**

Dan Patch, horizontal box, $6 \times 4 \times 2$ inches, **$35.**

Derby, horizontal box, 6 × 2 × 6½ inches,
$20.

Defender, horizontal box, 3 × 2 × 3 inches,
$225.

Diamond, horizontal box, 3 × 1 × ½ inches,
$45.

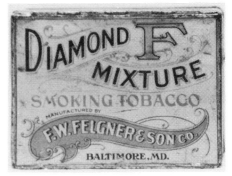

Diamond, horizontal box, 4 × 3 × 2 inches,
$45.

Dill's Best, horizontal box, 4 × 4 × 2 inches,
$15.

Dill's Best, horizontal box, 6 × 3 × 3 inches,
$15.

Dixie, barrel, 4½×2½ inches, **$250.**

Dixie, horizontal box, 4×3×1 inches, **$50.**

Doctor's Blend, horizontal box, 4×3×3 inches, **$25.**

Dulcet, horizontal box, 2×1½×½ inches, **$45.**

Echo, vertical box, 6×6×3 inches, **$100.**

1860, vertical box, 4×3×1 inches, **$450.**

Electric Mixture, horizontal box, 4×3×2 inches, **$450.**

English Bird's Eye, vertical box, $5 \times 3 \times 1$ inches, **$45.**

English Bird's Eye, horizontal box, $4 \times 2\frac{1}{2} \times 1\frac{1}{2}$ inches, **$45.**

English Slice, horizontal box, $6 \times 2 \times 1\frac{1}{2}$ inches, **$20.**

Enoch Arden, horizontal box, paper label, $3 \times 2 \times 1\frac{1}{2}$ inches, **$250.**

Ensign, horizontal box, $3 \times 1 \times 1$ inches, **$25.**

Epicure, horizontal box, $3 \times 3 \times 4$ inches, **$20.**

Epicure, casket, 8×5×4 inches, **$25.**

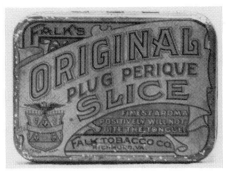

Falks, horizontal box, 4×3×1 inches, **$25.**

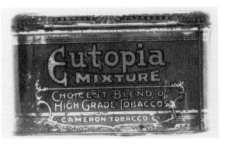

Eutopia, horizontal box, 6×4×4 inches, **$200.**

Famosa, horizontal box, 4×3×2 inches, **$90.**

Every Day, horizontal box, 4×3×1 inches, **$450.**

Fast Mail, horizontal box, 3×1×½ inches, **$200.**

Falk, horizontal box, 7×5×4 inches, **$90.**

Foursome, horizontal box, 3½×2½×1 inches, **$90.**

183

Fox's Mixture, vertical box, paper label, 4×3×2 inches, **$225.**

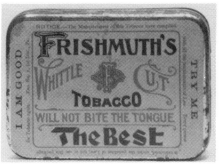

Frishmuth's, horizontal box, 4×3×1 inches, **$25.**

Friendship, horizontal box, 3½×1½×½ inches, **$25.**

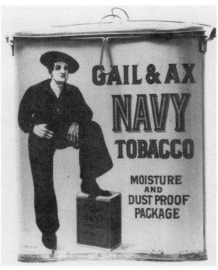

Gail & Ax Navy, store tin, irregular size, **$1,000+.**

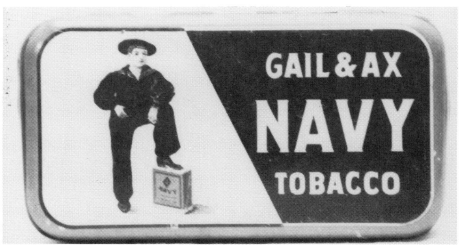

Gail & Ax Navy, horizontal box, 4×3×1 inches, **$30.**

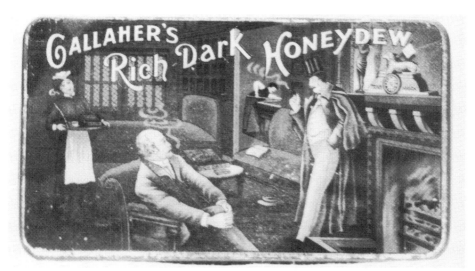

Gallaher's, horizontal box, $2 \times 1 \times \frac{1}{2}$ inches, **$25.**

Game, store tin, $24 \times 10 \times 12$ inches, **$450.**

Globe, horizontal box, $3 \times 1\frac{1}{2} \times \frac{1}{2}$ inches,
$85.

185

Globe, horizontal box, 5×5×3 inches, **$95.**

Gold Cross, horizontal box, 5×3×3 inches, **$30.**

Gold Medal, horizontal box, 4×2×½ inches, **$95.**

Golden Butterfly, horizontal box, 6×3×2 inches, **$25.**

Golden Crest, horizontal box, 4×2×2 inches, **$50.**

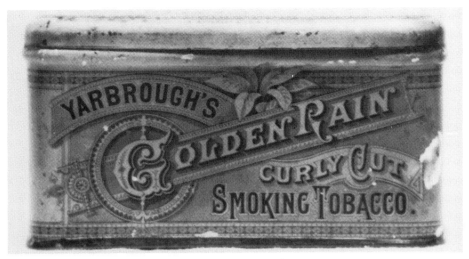

Golden Rain, horizontal box, 5 × 2 × 2½ inches, **$50.**

Golden Rod, horizontal box, 4 × 3 × 1 inches, **$95.**

Golden Square Cut, horizontal box, 4 × 3 × 1 inches, **$25.**

Golden Sceptre, horizontal box, 5 × 5 × 5 inches, **$25.**

Golden Thread, horizontal box, 3 × 2 × 1 inches, **$195.**

Golden Wedding, horizontal box, $4 \times 3 \times 1$ inches, **$45.**

Greek Slave, horizontal box, $4 \times 3 \times 1\frac{1}{2}$ inches, **$475.**

Great Store, horizontal box, $5 \times 4 \times 1$ inches, **$50.**

Green Goose, horizontal box, $6 \times 5 \times 3$ inches, **$900.**

Great West, horizontal box, $4 \times 6 \times 3$ inches, **$25.**

Green Seal, horizontal box, $3 \times 2 \times 2$ inches, **$95.**

Grouse-Moor, horizontal box, $3 \times 2 \times 1$ inches, **$25.**

Grizzly, horizontal box, paper label, $6 \times 4 \times 3$ inches, **$60.**

Handsome Dan, horizontal box, $7 \times 6 \times 2$ inches, **$95.**

Hard A Port, horizontal box, paper label, $6 \times 4 \times 3$ inches, **$95.**

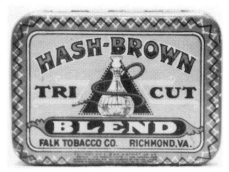

Hash Brown, horizontal box, $3 \times 2\frac{1}{2} \times 1$ inches, **$50.**

Highest Grade, horizontal box, $7 \times 4 \times 4$ inches, **$50.**

Hess & Co., horizontal box, $3\frac{1}{2} \times 1\frac{1}{2} \times \frac{1}{2}$ inches, **$750.**

Hignett's, horizontal box, $3 \times 2 \times 1$ inches, **$45.**

Hiawatha, horizontal box, $4 \times 2 \times 1\frac{1}{2}$ inches, **$25.**

Honest Labor, horizontal box, $4 \times 2 \times 1$ inches, **$20.**

High Card, flat round, 3×1 inches, **$25.**

Honest Scrap, store tin, 15×12×10 inches, **$1,000 +**.

Houde's No. 1, trunk, 12×6×3 inches, **$25.**

Huntoon, horizontal box, 4×3×1 inches, **$50.**

Hugh Campbell's, vertical box, 6×5×3 inches, **$100.**

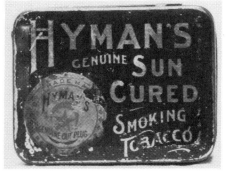

Hyman's, horizontal box, 4×3×2 inches, **$25.**

Idle Hour, horizontal box, 4 × 2 × ½ inches, **$20.**

Imperial Bird's Eye, vertical box, 5 × 2½ × 1½ inches, **$45.**

Imperial Smoking Mixture, horizontal box, 4 × 3 × ½ inches, **$15.**

Island, vertical box, 5 × 3 × 1½ inches, **$400.**

J.B. Pace, horizontal box, $6 \times 4 \times 2$ inches, **$50.**

J.G. Dill's, horizontal box, $4 \times 3 \times 1$ inches, **$90.**

Jewel of Virginia, horizontal box, $3 \times 2 \times 1$ inches, **$20.**

J.G. Dill's, horizontal box, $4 \times 3 \times 2$ inches, **$85.**

Jewel of Virginia, horizontal box, $4 \times 2 \times 1$ inches, **$25.**

Jule Carrs, horizontal box, 4 × 3 × 1 inches, **$50.**

Kentucky Smile, sample, 2 × ½ × ¼ inches, **$400.**

Khaki, horizontal box, 4 × 3 × 1 inches, **$45.**

King of All, vertical box, paper label, 4 × 2 × 1 inches, **$300.**

Kipling, horizontal box, 4 × 2 × 1 inches, **$35.**

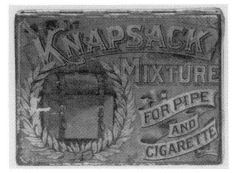

Knapsack, horizontal box, 4 × 3 × 1 inches, **$45.**

L.A.W., horizontal box, $4 \times 2 \times \frac{1}{2}$ inches, **$400**.

Labor King, horizontal box, $6 \times 4 \times 3$ inches, **$25**.

Life Boat, horizontal box, $3 \times 1 \times 3$ inches, **$45**.

Little Teazer Twist, horizontal box, $12 \times 6 \times 3$ inches, **$450**.

Lone Hand, horizontal box, $3\frac{1}{2} \times 1\frac{1}{2} \times \frac{1}{2}$ inches, **$240**.

Lone Jack, horizontal box, $4 \times 2 \times 1$ inches, **$25**.

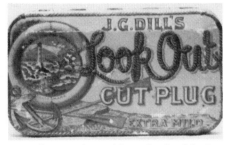

Look Out, horizontal box, $6 \times 3 \times 3$ inches, **$450**.

Lord Baltimore, horizontal box, $6 \times 4 \times 1$ inches, **$95**.

Louisiana Perique, horizontal box,
$3 \times 2 \times 1\frac{1}{2}$ inches, **$25.**

Lovell's Extra, horizontal box, $5 \times 4 \times 2$ inches, **$50.**

Loyal Fan, vertical box, $3\frac{1}{2} \times 3 \times \frac{1}{2}$ inches,
$50.

Lucky Cut Plug, vertical box, paper label,
$5 \times 4 \times 3$ inches, **$95.**

Lucky Strike, horizontal box, 4×3×4 inches, **$240.**

Lucky Strike, horizontal box, 4×3×1 inches, **$25.**

Lucky Strike, horizontal box, 3×2×1 inches, **$15.**

Madeira, horizontal box, 3×2×½ inches, **$75.**

Lucky Strike, horizontal box, 4×2×1 inches, **$18.**

Maryland Club, store tin, 15×10½×8 inches, **$500.**

Maryland Club, horizontal box, 3 × 2 × 1 inches, **$15.**

Master Workman, horizontal box, 4 × 2 × ½ inches, **$45.**

Mayo's Sliced Plug, horizontal box, 4 × 2 × 1 inches, **$25.**

Matador, horizontal box, 3 × 2 × 1½ inches, **$50.**

Mayo's Mixture, horizontal box, 4 × 3 × 1 inches, **$45.**

May Queen, horizontal box, 3 × 1 × ½ inches, **$250.**

Mayo's, horizontal box, 6×4×2 inches, **$25.**

McGill Mixture, horizontal box, 6×4×3 inches, **$45.**

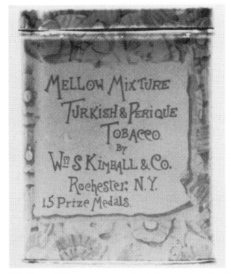

Mellow Mixture, vertical box, 4×2×2 inches, **$25.**

Mecca, horizontal box, 4×3×2 inches, **$25.**

Mellow Smoke, horizontal box, 4×2×1 inches, **$25.**

Monopol, horizontal box, 6 × 4 × 1 inches, **$50.**

Monte Cristo, horizontal box, 3 × 2 × 1 inches, **$25.**

Native, horizontal box, 3 × 2 × 1½ inches, **$50.**

Natalie, horizontal box, 4 × 4 × 1 inches, **$90.**

North Pole, horizontal box, 4×6×3 inches, **$50.**

North Pole, horizontal box, 6×4×4 inches, **$250.**

North Star, vertical box, 4×3×1 inches, **$250.**

North Star, horizontal box, 3×1×½ inches, **$475.**

O.K., horizontal box, 4×3×2½ inches, **$90.**

Oceanic, horizontal box, 4×6×2 inches, **$45.**

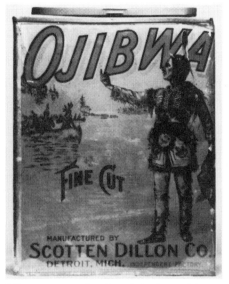

Ojibwa, store tin, 14×8 inches, **$250.**

Old Abe, horizontal box, 3×1½×½ inches, **$850.**

Old Abe, flat round, 2×8 inches, **$900.**

Old Colony, horizontal box, 4×3×3 inches, **$50.**

Old English, store tin, 24×15×12 inches, **$225.**

Old English, horizontal box, $3\frac{1}{2} \times 3 \times 1$ inches, **$15.**

Old Pop Smith, horizontal box, $3 \times 2 \times 1$ inches, **$100.**

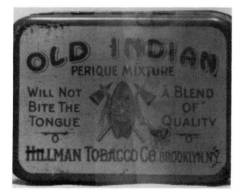

Old Indian, horizontal box, paper label, $4 \times 3 \times 2$ inches, **$25.**

Old Lady, horizontal box, $4 \times 3 \times 1$ inches, **$25.**

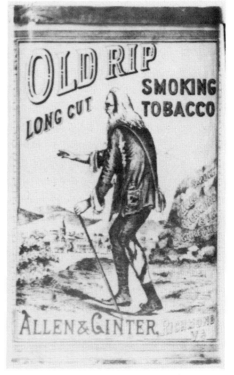

Old Rip, vertical box, $8 \times 3 \times 2$ inches, **$250.**

204

On the Square, square flat, $2 \times 2 \times \frac{1}{4}$ inches, **$20.**

Our Chums, horizontal box, $3 \times 1 \times 1\frac{1}{2}$ inches, **$25.**

Our Key West, horizontal box, $4 \times 3 \times 2$ inches, **$25.**

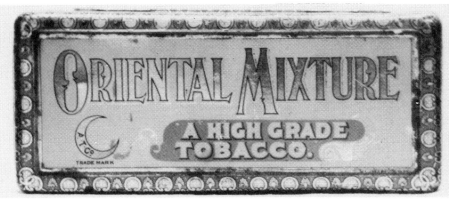

Oriental Mixture, horizontal box, $6 \times 3 \times \frac{1}{2}$ inches, **$25.**

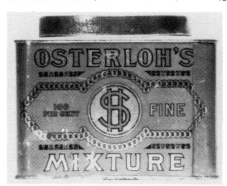

Osterloh's, horizontal box, $6 \times 4 \times 5$ inches, **$50.**

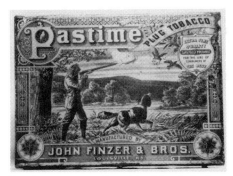

Pastime, store tin, $14 \times 10 \times 3$ inches, **$125.**

205

Patterson's Seal, vertical box, $6 \times 4 \times 4$ inches, **$25.**

Penn's, horizontal box, $5 \times 5 \times 2$ inches, **$25.**

Peter Hauptmann, horizontal box, $3 \times 2 \times 1$ inches, **$45.**

Piccadilly, horizontal box, $4 \times 3 \times 1$ inches, **$20.**

Peculiar, triangular shape, $5 \times 1 \times 1$ inches, **$100.**

Perique Unadulterated, horizontal box, $3 \times 2 \times 1$ inches, **$45.**

Piper Heidsieck, horizontal box, $8 \times 3 \times 3$ inches, **$30.**

Pig Skin, oval, football-shaped, **$500.**

Piper Heidsieck, square flat, $2 \times 2 \times \frac{1}{4}$ inches, **$10.**

Pilot Flake, horizontal box, $5 \times 3 \times 2$ inches, **$50.**

Player's, horizontal box, 2½ × 1 × ¾ inches, **$15.**

Plow Boy, store tin, 15 × 15 × 20 inches, **$475.**

Poet's Dream, horizontal box, 3 × 2 × 1½ inches, **$25.**

Poker, horizontal box, 6 × 4 × 3 inches, **$225.**

Poker, horizontal box, 4 × 3 × 1 inches, **$375.**

Pride of the East, horizontal box, 4 × 2 × 1 inches, **$50.**

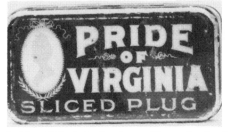

Pride of Virginia, horizontal box, 4 × 2 × 1 inches, **$10.**

Princess Royal, vertical box, $5 \times 3 \times 1\frac{1}{2}$ inches, **$50.**

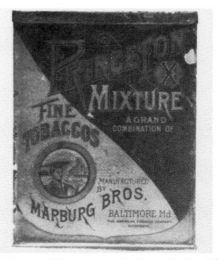

Princeton Mixture, vertical box, $4 \times 3 \times 1\frac{1}{2}$ inches, **$100.**

Prize Winners, horizontal box, $4 \times 3 \times 1$ inches, **$50.**

Prune Nugget, horizontal box, $6 \times 3 \times 2$ inches, **$50.**

Puritan, horizontal box, $6 \times 4 \times 2$ inches, **$50.**

Q Boid, vertical box, $4 \times 3 \times 2$ inches, **$25.**

Rainbow, horizontal box, $6 \times 6 \times 3$ inches, **$100.**

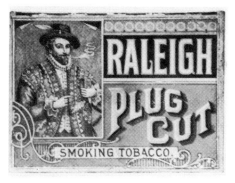

Raleigh, vertical box, paper label, $4\frac{1}{2} \times 3\frac{1}{2} \times 2$ inches, **$175.**

Ram's Horn, horizontal box, $4 \times 2 \times 1$ inches, **$100.**

Raptco, horizontal box, $2 \times 1 \times \frac{1}{2}$ inches, **$10.**

Real Thing, horizontal box, $4 \times 6 \times 2$ inches, **$50.**

Red Indian, horizontal box, paper label, 6 × 4 × 2 inches, **$100.**

Redbreast, horizontal box, 2 × 2 × 1 inches, **$50.**

Red Label, horizontal box, 4 × 2 × 1 inches, **$50.**

Repeater, horizontal box, 3 × 4 × 2 inches, **$35.**

Red J, horizontal box, 6 × 6 × 3 inches, **$90.**

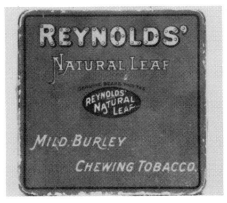

Reynolds', horizontal box, 3½ × 3 × ½ inches, **$25.**

Richmond Belle, horizontal box, $4 \times 3 \times 2$ inches, **$500.**

Richmond Star, horizontal box, $4 \times 3 \times 2$ inches, **$95.**

Richmond Belle, horizontal box, $4 \times 3 \times 1$ inches, **$10.**

Richmond Gem, horizontal box, $4 \times 3 \times 1$ inches, **$50.**

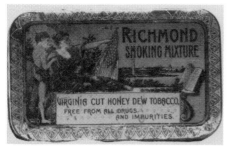

Richmond, horizontal box, $5 \times 3 \times 1\frac{1}{2}$ inches, **$95.**

Richmond Best, horizontal box, $4 \times 4 \times 3$ inches, **$25.**

212

Richmond Mixture, horizontal box, 3×2×2 inches, **$25.**

Rod & Reel, horizontal box, 4×3×1 inches, **$50.**

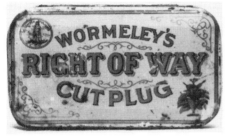

Right of Way, horizontal box, 4×2×1 inches, **$50.**

Saffa Mixture, horizontal box, 4×3×1 inches, **$40.**

Salmagundi, vertical box, 3×2×2 inches, **$45.**

Ringer's, vertical box, 5×3×3 inches, **$50.**

Santa Clara, horizontal box, $6 \times 4 \times 2$ inches, **$50.**

Seal Rock, horizontal box, $4 \times 3 \times 2$ inches, **$100.**

Saratoga Chips, horizontal box, $4 \times 2\frac{1}{2} \times 1$ inches, **$10.**

Senator, horizontal box, $5 \times 4 \times 3$ inches, **$25.**

Saratoga Tabac, trunk-shaped, $12 \times 8 \times 4$ inches, **$25.**

Sensible, horizontal box, $4 \times 3 \times 2$ inches, **$10.**

Seal of North Carolina, horizontal box, $4 \times 3 \times 1$ inches, **$50.**

Shakespeare, horizontal box, $4 \times 3 \times 2$ inches, **$200.**

Sphinx, horizontal box, $4 \times 3 \times 1$ inches, **$40.**

Shandigaf, horizontal box, $4 \times 3 \times \frac{1}{2}$ inches, **$50.**

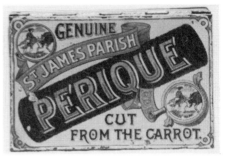

St. James Parish Perique, horizontal box, $3 \times 2 \times 1$ inches, **$100.**

Silver Dell, horizontal box, $4 \times 3 \times 2$ inches, **$50.**

St. Leger Oval, horizontal box, $5 \times 3 \times 1$ inches, **$50.**

Spanish Puffs, horizontal box, $4 \times 3 \times 2$ inches, **$20.**

St. Leger, horizontal box, $2\frac{1}{2} \times 1\frac{1}{2} \times \frac{1}{2}$ inches, **$10.**

Sultan's, horizontal box, $5 \times 3 \times 3$ inches, **$50.**

Stag, horizontal box, $5 \times 5 \times 5$ inches, **$50.**

Sun Cured, horizontal box, $4 \times 6 \times 3$ inches, **$200.**

Staple Mixture, horizontal box, $5\frac{1}{2} \times 3\frac{1}{2} \times 2$ inches, **$50.**

Sun Flower, horizontal box, $4 \times 3 \times 1$ inches, **$800.**

Superior, horizontal box, $3 \times 2 \times \frac{1}{2}$ inches, **$10.**

Surbrugs, horizontal box, $6 \times 3 \times 4$ inches, **$50.**

Sure Shot, store tin, $20 \times 8 \times 6$ inches, **$250.**

Sweet Caporal, horizontal box, $3 \times 2 \times 1$ inches, **$45.**

Sweet Cuba, store tin, $36 \times 20 \times 20$ inches, **$250.**

Sweet Clover, horizontal box, $3 \times 2 \times \frac{1}{2}$ inches, **$200.**

217

Sweet Cuba, store tin, 12×8 inches, **$100.**

Sweet Cuba, store tin, cardboard label, 12×8 inches, **$100.**

Sweet Mist, store tin, cardboard label, 12×7×5 inches, **$100.**

Tally Ho, horizontal box, 3½×1½×½ inches, **$225.**

Temple Bar, horizontal box, 2½×2½×½ inches, **$25.**

Three States, oval flat, $\frac{1}{2} \times 4\frac{1}{2} \times 2$ inches, **$350.**

Three States, horizontal box, $4 \times 3 \times 2$ inches, **$25.**

Three Twins, horizontal box, $5 \times 2 \times 1\frac{1}{2}$ inches, **$250.**

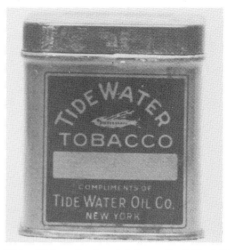

Tide Water, horizontal box, $2 \times 1\frac{1}{2} \times 1\frac{1}{2}$ inches, **$50.**

Tiger, store tin, cardboard, $12 \times 8 \times 5$ inches, **$100.**

Tiger Brand, horizontal box, 5×3×1 inches, **$45.**

Tin Tag Plug, horizontal box, 15×3×½ inches, **$400.**

Tiger, horizontal box, 3×1½×½ inches, **$35.**

Tonka, horizontal box, 5×4×3 inches, **$85.**

Topaz, horizontal box, $4 \times 3 \times 2$ inches, **$25.**

Turkish Mixture, horizontal box, $3 \times 2 \times 1\frac{1}{2}$ inches, **$45.**

Tortoise Shell, horizontal box, $3 \times 1\frac{1}{2} \times 1$ inches, **$225.**

Turkish, horizontal box, $3 \times 2 \times 1\frac{1}{2}$ inches, **$45.**

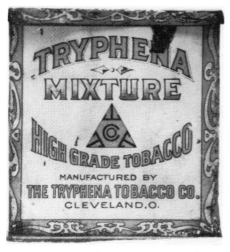

Tryphena, vertical box, $4 \times 3\frac{1}{2} \times 1\frac{1}{2}$ inches, **$25.**

Tuxedo, horizontal box, $6 \times 4 \times 4$ inches, **$90.**

Tuxedo, vertical box, $4 \times 2 \times 2$ inches, **$80.**

Twenty One, horizontal box, $4 \times 4 \times 1$ inches, **$240.**

Two Eleven, horizontal box, paper label, $3 \times 2\frac{1}{2} \times \frac{1}{2}$ inches, **$25.**

Tuxedo, vertical box, $5 \times 4 \times 2$ inches, **$20.**

Twin Oaks, casket, $8 \times 4 \times 4$ inches, **$65.**

Uniform, horizontal box, 6×4×3 inches, **$225.**

Union Leader, horizontal box, 4×6×3 inches, **$20.**

University of Michigan, vertical box, 4×3×2 inches, **$225.**

University of Chicago, horizontal box, 4×3×2 inches, **$225.**

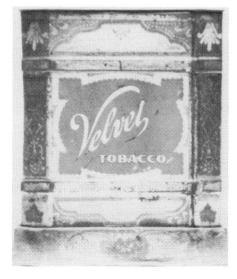

Velvet, octagonal shape, 6×4 inches, **$35.**

Velvet, octagonal shape, 4×3 inches, **$40.**

Virginia Dare, horizontal box, 4×3×1 inches, **$90.**

Vim, horizontal box, 3×2×1 inches, **$50.**

Virginia Flakes, horizontal box, 4×3×1 inches, **$40.**

Virginia Creeper, horizontal box, 4×3×2 inches, **$400.**

Virginians, horizontal box, 4×1½×½ inches, **$95.**

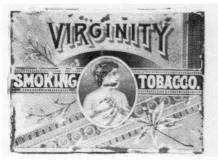

Virginity, horizontal box, 8×5×5 inches, **$150.**

Virginity, horizontal box, 4×3×2 inches, **$50.**

Ward's Best, horizontal box, paper label, 6×6×3 inches, **$50.**

Whip, octagonal shape, 6×5 inches, **$200.**

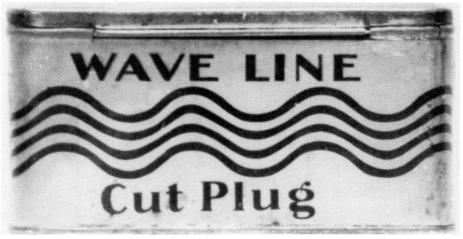

Wave Line, horizontal box, paper label, 6×4×2 inches, **$50.**

Willoughby Taylor, horizontal box, 6×6×4 inches, **$20.**

White House, horizontal box, 4½×3×2 inches, **$65.**

Worker, horizontal box, 4×6×3 inches, **$85.**

William Penn, horizontal box, paper label, 4×3×2 inches, **$50.**

Wild Fruit, horizontal box, 4×6×3 inches, **$30.**

World's Navy, horizontal box, $8 \times 8 \times 3$ inches, **$25.**

World's Standard, horizontal box, $4 \times 3 \times 1$ inches, **$50.**

Yale, horizontal box, $4 \times 3 \times 2$ inches, **$15.**

Yale, horizontal box, $4 \times 2 \times \frac{1}{2}$ inches, **$95.**

Yankee Slice, horizontal box, $3\frac{1}{2} \times 3\frac{1}{2}$ inches, **$25.**

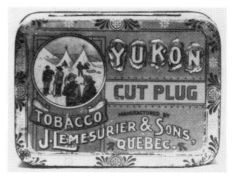

Yukon, horizontal box, $4 \times 3 \times 2$ inches, **$300.**

Yoc-O-May, horizontal box, 4×2×1 inches, **$30.**

Revised Prices

231